Simple Rustic Furniture

Simple
Rustic
Furniture

A Weekend Workshop
with Dan Mack

Daniel Mack

LARK BOOKS
ASHEVILLE, NORTH CAROLINA

EDITOR:
DEBORAH MORGENTHAL

ART DIRECTOR:
CHRIS BRYANT

PRODUCTION ASSISTANT:
HANNES CHAREN

PHOTOGRAPHY:
JONATHAN WALLEN

ILLUSTRATIONS:
JENNIFER ZELMAN

ADDITIONAL PHOTOGRAPHY:
Bob Barret, Ron Cedar,
Bobby Hansson, David Horton,
Daniel Mack, Rita Nicholas,
SRC, and Nick Zungoli

Library of Congress Cataloging-in-Publication Data
Mack, Daniel, 1947–
    Simple rustic furniture : a weekend workshop
with Dan Mack / by Daniel Mack.—1st ed.
     p.   cm.
   Includes index.
   ISBN 1-57990-086-0 (hardcover)
    1. Rustic woodwork. 2. Furniture making.
  3. Country furniture. I. Title
TT200.M22 1999
684.1'.04—dc21   98-34719
                                   CIP

10 9 8 7 6 5 4 3 2 1

First Edition

Published by Lark Books
50 College St.
Asheville, NC 28801
USA

© 1999, Daniel Mack

Distributed by Random House, Inc.,
in the United States, Canada, the United Kingdom, Europe, and Asia

Distributed in Australia by Capricorn Link (Australia) Pty Ltd.,
P.O. Box 6651, Baulkham Hills Business Centre, NSW 2153, Australia

Distributed in New Zealand by Tandem Press Ltd.,
2 Rugby Rd., Birkenhead, Auckland, New Zealand

Printed in Hong Kong
by Oceanic Graphic Printing Productions, Ltd.

ACKNOWLEDGMENTS

I appreciate the many other rustics who keep in touch with me through letters, calls and e-mail. Their pictures and stories have helped me deepen my understanding of the vitality, creativity, and regenerative nature of working with natural forms.

CONTENTS

WELCOME, WEEKEND RUSTIC!

Daniel Mack with two of his chairs. PHOTO BY DAVID HORTON

Illustration, titled "Up in the Crow's Nest," from an 1850s Harper's Weekly

Twenty years ago, tucked away in a maple grove on Round Top Mountain in the Catskill Mountains, I built my first rustic chair. I can still remember my amazement when the crude, whittled tenons and the mortises started fitting together, and a chair-shaped object began to appear. I was a Weekend Rustic! My enthusiasm for this style of furniture has only grown. I have become a kind of missionary, encouraging everybody and anybody to find pleasure and self-expression by working with the trees.

You need not be experienced with tools; you may not be looking for a new career. But if you have a few hours or an open weekend, this book can be your guide. For those of you who want to "build," I'm eager to share the few simple techniques I've been using for the past 20 years. For those of you who want to watch, dream, collect, sketch, paint, arrange, or admire—this book is for you, too.

Building has always been a mystery to me, and I've tried to protect that feeling because I enjoy not knowing exactly how something will turn out before I start. I enjoy the edge of discomfort that comes with not having a set of plans. There's a part of me that perhaps looks forward to the possibility of failure. That's one reason the plans, the preparation, the cut list, the interlocking elements of construction, have always made me shrink from a "building project." But I've also learned that even more than the possibility of failure, there is the possibility of discovery—of the right sticks, in the right combination. Rustic work seems to offer a form of adventure I like. It doesn't all have to be involved with "building."

Sometimes I just go to the woods. Period. I don't have a "cut list." I haven't made future plans for what this trip to the woods might yield; I don't know. There is pleasure in sitting, breathing, walking, searching, finding, discovering.

I might return with a bit of moss or a fern for my yard, or a stone or a bone or a skeletal leaf. These treasures find their way around my home: onto shelves, dressers, nightstands, window sills...into the quiet daily shrines we all make for ourselves. These are as important as any chair or table. They share the same vitality as the sticks...they feed us in their own special way. It's important to remember the modest uses of natural forms, especially as we now prepare to fill spaces with our grand gestures of fences, arbors, ladders, and settees.

When I first started making rustic furniture in 1978, it was weekend work. It was fun, a relief from the other work I was doing. I looked for things to make that I could start and finish in a weekend or two, and, importantly, with tools and materials I had around.

This book is about a particular approach to making things. I did not grow up "handy." I'm still not very handy. I improvise. I cook the way I build and build the way I cook. I use the tools of the kitchen, ingredients that are available, but usually no recipe; I cook by color, favorite spice, ingredient of the moment. And I get an interesting dinner on the table every night. I inherited this from my grandfather: he tinkered, too. His way seeped into me and came out years later as rustic furniture.

One thing I've learned from 10 years of teaching rustic work is that each of us brings to the branches and the tools a lifetime of habits and attitudes just waiting to be released into the furniture. That's the extra lure of this work: it reveals something about ourselves.

1930s postcard of a rustic bridge in California

ABOVE: Student fitting pieces together to form a chair.
PHOTO BY DAVID HORTON

LEFT: Abby trying out a rustic bassinet made by Daniel Mack

Laura Spector's vine bench— serene at the beach and alive with children

Jeff Snyder's work captures the power and fluid movement of the white water he loves to ride.

There is something magical, mystical, invigorating about the Act of Making—in the thinking, arranging of time, gathering of materials and tools, clearing of space, the bravery of cutting and assembly, the revising and reworking. In the muscularity and public quality of the act, there is something fundamental, historical, prehistorical, archetypal. In the act of making, we are saying—in body and space and material—that we exist. Making is a form of expression.

Making with natural materials is an enriched form of expression. We are not only engaged in the physical and emotional process of creating, but we are literally in touch, in collaboration with other natural forces. By including and celebrating the grown shape of the stick or the worn surface of the rock, we are taking part in a very old tradition.

Rustic woodworking offers an encounter with the raw, the testy. It makes you confront design and beauty in your own way. You have to be an inventor. It's a very brisk experience. You get to know more about trees and yourself. It's the opportunity to ignore rules, change rules, and make up new ones.

The Weekend Rustic has an advantage over the Vocational Rustic. My making is clouded with the marketplace: trends, tastes, prices, shows, shipping. I'm tethered in a way a Weekend Rustic like you is not. You can think, gather, and make with a trance-like idyll. You can allow yourself the luxury of enjoying the act, the process of making, with little regard for the outcome. If a bench appears at the end of this, all the better—or so what? You have the pleasure of waking up to an indistinct day, the search, the hunt for the materials…the touching of the wood…its firmness, wetness. You celebrate the ritual of harvesting the wood.

You sit quietly in the woods and then say a few words to the trees to join you to them. Or perhaps you stay distant, looking and moving in, like the lion to the prey. You relish the smell of the wood and the woods: one fresh, the other ancient decay. You are busy trimming the wood and dragging it out; you are occupied with decisions about sizing and loading and securing the wood for the trip home. Then you face the unloading and carrying, the storing, and waiting for the wood to dry. It's very likely that you have left sweat, and even blood, on the trees. You probably smell, and maybe you got into poison ivy, and maybe you found an animal skull, and maybe you lost your tape measure. You have had an exchange.

You have spent part of yourself...on what? Something elusive, an idyll. You have plowed into a new world—probably a slower, more textural world. You are pioneering!

Be prepared to meet Jack's mother...and maybe even the Giant. If you dare to make some rustic furniture, people will talk. More than talk, they'll have some very pointed comments and opinions. Enjoy them.

Oh no, you've sold the cow for a handful of beans!

What cow? You could have been cutting the grass, weeding the garden, planting the garden, washing the car, painting the back of the house, reading a book, going to a soccer game, doing the laundry.

What beans? This dumb pile of sticks is not even dry enough for kindling!

ABOVE: Driftwood poles await students at a rustic course at the Omega Institute in New York.
PHOTO BY DAVID HORTON

LEFT: Dirk Leach's rare photograph of "where baby trees come from"

BELOW: Birch presentation plaque by Steven Walsh

Alan Bradstreet built this chair with found objects.

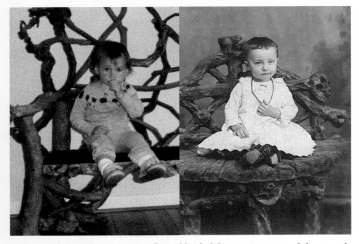
Children and rustic furniture are a fitting blend of the spontaneous and the eternal.

Father and son spent a weekend together while dad built this chair at a workshop.

We don't really need an arbor. A chair? For where? When will it be done? **When?** Jack's mother lives in all of us. But Jack knew how to make time and space for himself. And, actually, if Jack's mother hadn't thrown those beans outside, there'd be no beanstalk.

As a weekend maker you don't need to tally up items per hour. You have the opportunity to practice something very ancient: you can shapeshift…take on a new form. You can become in-spired…literally filled with air. Your movements will be quite different from those of your weekday life. You might move faster, might seem, sound, and look more like a dancer, a singer, a poet. You may seem silly, childlike. That's a good sign.

For you, the Weekend Builder, rustic making can be an adjective to life, something that describes and elaborates who you are and what you do. It can become a quality you have and display. It's not a central noun, like it is for us Business Builders. You have the luxury of play, of making gifts, of making folly. Much of the work in this book was created by other weekend rustics. They may want to make a living at rustic work, but it hasn't yet happened. Their work still retains the charm and glow of work protected from the wear of the marketplace.

Rustic furniture seems to find its way into life's ceremonies. It's good for family photos; to mark a special event: a birthday, a marriage, a party. That's because it's unusual, recognizably tied to nature and the product of a human hand working in slow deliberate time.

Rustic work has always been rooted in the slow and casual. It was winter work, and still is, for many builders in the construction trades. It's often seen as work for "retirement," an offensive term for that time of life when people usually get more control over what they do and can actually develop new ways of growing in skill and self-expression.

Let me end this introduction by relating the story of a long-gone weekend rustic, George Carr, of Union Springs, New York. That's in the Finger Lakes region, where I grew up.

George Carr was a Civil War veteran and a multi-talented man. He was a farmer, a musician, and a wood-carver. In 1911, when he was 70 years old, he started to "spruce up" his homestead with carvings on dead trees, stumps, stones, and fence posts. He made rustic benches and other "curious" things. For the next 14 years, he carved and painted dozens of objects that all started with the twist of the tree, the burrow of the insect.

Thousands of people came to see his work. In 1923, he sold 7,000 postcards of his most famous work, The Totem Tree. Today, nothing is left of his work but these pictures. George Carr was a good weekend rustic. He was in touch with nature, and he recognized and honored his own need to fashion, to make something in collaboration with the accidents of nature and weather. He was willing to have his creations, his oddities, seen by the public, and in that he inspired others to take the risk to make particular, peculiar things.

Today, there are more George Carrs than ever still making "curiosities." Join them!

In 1922, George Carr and his wife posed alongside his famous Totem Tree.

Jack Sewall and one of his garden twig creatures

The Types of Rustic Makers

YOU MAY RECOGNIZE PARTS OF YOURSELF IN THESE DESCRIPTIONS OF THE DIFFERENT WAYS OF BEING—AND BEING RUSTIC.

The Hunter: You are active, moving, dynamic, seeking the unknown. You have a short, intense attention span; you want results. You enjoy the search and the discovery. You need the chance of utter failure to be a success. You can search the local woods for new materials to add to your storehouse. Odd shapes, supple branches, more driftwood, mosses. You remember where things are and how to get there; you might make a map. You like to create, extend, and defend.

The Muse: You find the trees to fit the air. You make music with trees. You make dance with branches; you make sculpture and shadows. Your work is beautifully insubstantial. You have come from Mnemosyne, the source of deep memory. So time, slow time, is a part of your work. You use the musky smells of the forest in your work.

The Bodger: You use the tools in cooperation with the trees so that both the tree and the maker can be recognized. You saw, drill, whittle, sand, glue, peg. You come from the line of Hephestus—the inventor, the craftsman who was kicked off Olympus and kept trying to invent ways back. You know ways of protecting and providing comfort. You build chairs, tables, tools, shelters, huts, and lean-tos.

The Magician: You study the sticks and hold the sticks and decide what sticks are right for being special. You reveal and release the power in sticks by choosing, placing, sanding, whittling, coloring, and giving the sticks to others. You might tell about secret places and ways. You are compelled to make things special. You understand the unseen and unspoken around you. You see how sticks can become part of something else. You have a sense of patience and experimentation. You have a broad view. You know that things never stay the same.

WORKING WITH THE TREES

(Notes the author wrote about his recent work)

Working with Natural Forms

    offers reminders of mortality...

the chance to feel time-bound,

linked to the seasons, these woods,

the capillary action of water leaving wood...

Leaving wood available for its next life.

Shrinkage and expansion

    trough and peak

    co-equal partners in life

        the fleshy sounds

            of wetness

        the crisp sounds

            of dryness...

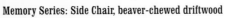

Memory Series: Side Chair, beaver-chewed driftwood

Counter stools, 34 inches high

Working with Natural Forms helps develop

tolerance and forgiveness

the appreciation of approximation

the celebration of differences

the value of deformities.

Working with Natural Forms

is a chance to explore rhythms,

magnify, modify, enhance common ones,

add new ones:

what are your rhythms?

you have a language

before you know

"grammar."

Dining chair, 47 inches high,
hand-shaped cherry,
lye treated, leather upholstery

Each tool,

each form,

each wood

has an inherent sense of time,

texture.

If objects have Soul...

tools do too...

There is an inherent danger—

often costing a drop of blood,

a stitch or two.

LEFT: Men's Dangling Chair, 12 inches high, maple
branches with fishing tackle. RIGHT: Don't Leave
Your Chair Outside, driftwood with wasps nests

ABOVE AND TOP OF FACING PAGE: Counter stools,
34 inches high with curved backs

LEFT: **Memory series:**
Garden Arm Chair,
63 inches high, maple
saplings and garden tools

We're hurt, chastened,

    and slowed down…

It hurts our sense of control, ambition.

It forces us to alter our plans…

Who can we blame? Nobody!

Just be available to the delight

    and weariness of

        frustration and discovery.

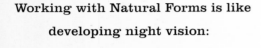

ABOVE AND BELOW: Staircase with driftwood logs, Westchester, New York, Daniel Mack

Working with Natural Forms is like

    developing night vision:

at first everything is quite Black…
then…dimension, depth appear.

This happens when there is both

  a shift

    in Light and Time and Space.

Working with Natural Forms

 is about Altered rhythms:

  can you just be with the materials—

without needing to rework them...quite yet.

The need to start reworking

 is like the need

  to turn the light on,

 to re-establish

  your sense of time.

Be Brave.

 See how long

  you can take

   the Altered State.

ABOVE: Peeled maple arm chair, 45 inches high, upholstered seat

BELOW: Apron table, 40 inches high, pine

Memory Series: Arm Chair, driftwood, found objects, upholstered seat

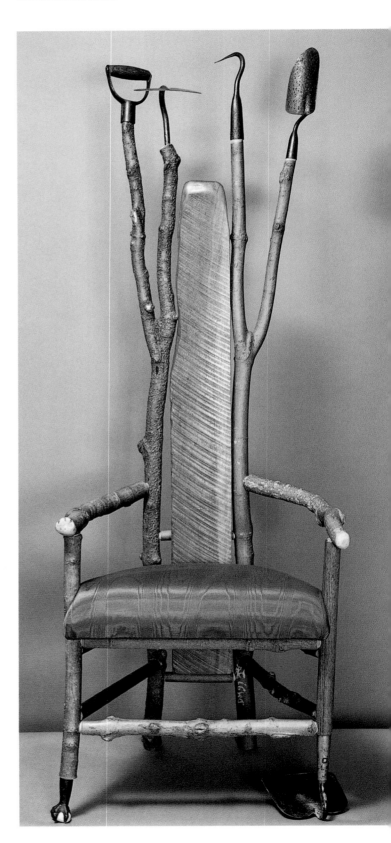

Working with Natural Forms is about

"never perfect enough"...

It makes you think and feel about

repaired, cobbled objects.

Working with Natural Forms is

a way to make the Sacred

from the Ordinary...

arranging, ritualizing objects.

BELOW AND PRECEEDING PAGE: Memory Series: Lord and Lady Dining Chairs, maple branches, cherry boards, found objects. PHOTO BY SRC

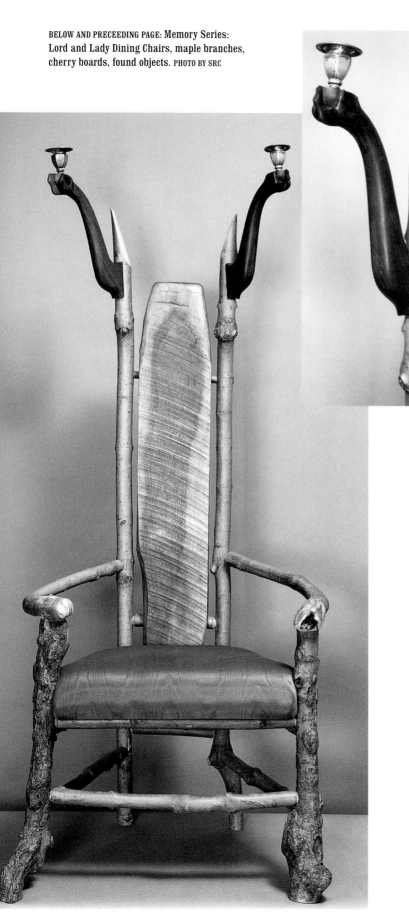

Religio means binding back,
    rejoining
It makes you think about joinery
    in a new way.

My work has been about retrieval
Bringing back a lost furniture form
Bringing myself back to a balance
Using objects, chair-trees
    to recall old stories
        which people already know…
            but may not have heard
                in a long time.

All art, poetry, dance does that…
    It more or less evokes
            Deep Memory,
            Mnemosyne.

Memory series: Croquet Desk Chair for Jonathan, maple branches and parts of antique croquet sets

Styles of Rustic Furniture

Philip Crandon, Andrea Franz

Stick or Twig

Stick or twig furniture is made from young trees and branches, connected in a manner that echoes their natural form. Despite its fragile appearance, stick furniture is sturdy enough for everyday use, if the pieces are cut fresh and then allowed to dry thoroughly. The wood can be used as is or peeled. This rustic style is spontaneous and interactive. Because there are few plans to follow and very little or no reshaping required, stick furniture is a good style for beginners. Whether the joints are nailed together, fastened with dowels, or glued with mortise and tenon joints, the challenge lies in selecting wood with the right proportions.

Trees and Logs

Tree or log furniture is stick furniture on a grand scale. Logs are good for constructing beds or outdoor seating. They're also used to build rustic gazebos, pergolas, and arbors. Although log furniture lacks the detail found in stick and twig furniture, it can be made with roots and burls, which will give the finished piece visual interest. For indoor furniture, lodgepole pine, aspen, and juniper are popular; white cedar is a good choice because it has low weight for its volume and is easy to work and finish. For outdoor work, black locust, white cedar, and redwood hold up well if peeled to minimize bug infestation.

Found and Salvaged Wood

Found and salvaged wood, such as chestnut logs, fence rails, and discarded wooden shipping materials (pallets), has become more and more the object of the rustic maker's imagination. By the time the rustic gets hold of it, the wood has already experienced a history of use—aside from being part of a tree. Many rustics reclaim wood from various parts of old houses or barns. Cheek cuts and irregular wood from sawmills are also good for combining with fresh-cut wood. Driftwood is coveted because of its naturally finished surfaces. Any wood left long enough in the hostile environment of oceans, lakes, or rivers will begin to lose hard edges and revert toward its original form.

Bentwood

Bentwood, a popular rustic style that involves careful planning, is created by bending and nailing long, straight, and thin branches or tree suckers around a sturdily built frame. Patience is required to shape the fresh wands of wood into graceful curves and other patterns. Builders of bentwood furniture can be found throughout the United States, wherever there are supple, fast-growing woods, such as willow, alder, or cottonwood.

Split Work, Mosaic, and Swiss Work

These three names denote the style in which full or half-rounded branches are nailed or glued over a wooden frame. This careful, often painstaking work, creates volume and intricacy, delicacy and geometry. A lavish visual variety can be created by using a variety of woods or different forms of the same species.

Bark Appliqué

Bark appliqué is a technique in which birch or cedar bark is appliquéd on top of existing casework. Many times, the edges of the surface are finished with Swiss work which functions to keep the bark from curling. Bark work is rarely used on chairs, but more commonly on cupboards, tables, desks, clocks, and picture frames. The bark for this rustic furniture is harvested twice a year in areas where durable white-paper birch, golden birch, and fire cherry are found.

Root and Burl Work

This rustic style creates furniture using intricate, dense root systems of trees and shrubs. The roots of mountain laurel, rhododendron, and juniper are traditional favorites for this type of rustic building. These materials are often found in the form of driftwood or discarded wood on land being cleared for development. Aesthetic and technical skills are required to successfully combine the gangly roots with other wood to make an appealing piece of furniture.

Burls, the wartlike knobs sometimes found on tree trunks and limbs, are natural growths formed by trees to protect or heal themselves. They are cherished for their unusual grain pattern and are often used in veneers. Some rustic builders split the burls and polish the grain face for use as a tabletop. Others use them as a design element in stick or log furniture.

MATERIALS, TECHNIQUES, AND TOOLS

This section discusses the finding, choosing, cutting, storing, and drying of materials; the various methods of joining the materials together; the tools available for accomplishing this joinery; and different ways of finishing the wood. Because rustic work has more to do with looking and dreaming than with measuring and planning, the information in this section has a somewhat circular and interlacing shape to it. I start out talking about materials, but can't help discussing something relevant about cutting. Or, when I finally say all I have to about tools, some of it may already sound familiar because of what I described about techniques.

This section mirrors how I make rustic furniture. The way in which I think about materials is related to where I can find them and how I need to cut them; how I choose to join the pieces to make, let's say, a chair, is an extension of the tools I like to use and what the wood looks like. Eventually I will deliver you to an intended destination, and you'll know what you need in order to make a table or a chair with the materials and tools of your choosing. But getting there may have some unexpected detours, recurring switchbacks, and, I hope, a few pleasant surprises.

MATERIALS

It's very likely that if you purchased this book you already have some of the pieces of the Weekend Rustic puzzle. You probably have wood squirreled away from a trip to the beach or the woods. You may have some tools you like working with. Maybe you sketched out an idea or clipped a photo from a magazine that shows one of your dream rustic projects. These are all anchor points for working with this book. Nonetheless, I'll go through all the various ingredients. If you have them, great; if you need some reminders, here they are.

Materials are the most distinguishing characteristic of rustic work. You, the Rustic, hunt for wood—not lumber—and leave it in the shapes and textures pretty much as you found it; you just change its lengths and the way it relates to other similar pieces of wood.

ANY NATURAL FORM MATERIAL WILL DO. ANY NATURAL FORM MATERIAL WILL DO...AGAIN?

You can make something from anything. So find a farmer with an overgrown field. Call a tree service company in your suburbs. Talk to your local Parks or Highway Department. Attend a Planning or Zoning Board meeting and meet developers. Call the local Extension Service and inquire about getting a cutting permit. Ask your neighbors what they're planning to trim or prune. Look in the back of this book for the names of materials suppliers. So now you've solved your access to the materials. That's the easy part.

ABOVE: Bench by
Maxwell Newhouse

RIGHT: Peeled pine
and bittersweet chair,
Tim Dibble

BELOW: Twig mosaic
bench, Todd Barrow

WHAT DO YOU WANT TO DO WITH THE MATERIALS?

It's likely that you have some thoughts about just what materials you think are most desirable. Preparing, sizing, and storing the materials are more difficult issues. If you like that Peeled Wood look, you're in for a lot of quiet time—you, the knife, and the branches. If you want to do mortise and tenon work (peg-in-hole joinery), you'll have to dry at least some of your wood pretty well before you use it. That means time...near the furnace, in a kiln, in a dry area somewhere. If you'd like to do something NOW, then go get a saw, a hammer and nails and you can work with wood so fresh it's still cool.

My point here is that Materials is a prism of the way you like to do things. It's a reflection of your particular ingenuity at finding something unusual, exercising your imagination, developing stamina, being resourceful at finding storage, deciding whether to wait to work the wood dry or actively tangle yourself up in a project right now.

The area of Materials will be approached differently by every single person. That simple word "materials" hides many different gremlins waiting to challenge each of us. They appear to say such things as:

> "You'll never find the right saplings to do this.
>
> The saplings you get will have bugs and rot and you'll poison everybody.
>
> Dan Mack has already used all the best saplings.
>
> You might get arrested.
>
> You will hurt yourself.
>
> This is a waste of time and everybody will laugh at you.
>
> You're just going to clutter up the house, the yard, the garage, and...
>
> There are better ways to spend your time."

My own gremlins usually play to my fear of a fatal, long-standing hidden flaw in my plans:

> "Oh sure, the materials look right, but just wait until you start to work with them or just wait until you bring the finished chair indoors, then you'll see. Fool!"

Gremlins are a fact of life, and must be recognized as such and worked with. Make a little gremlin chair or shrine. Every time you hear the gremlin voice coming in to demolish you and your project, put a few wood chips at the chair or shrine...or a bent nail or a drop of glue. Gremlins fall quiet for a while when they are recognized. **But they do not go away**.

DRYING YOUR WOOD

The key thing to remember is that you want to delay the process of the tree returning itself to the earth. The natural cycle for a tree is to appear, leaf out, produce seeds, go dormant—and then repeat this for its entire life cycle (which is usually longer than a human life). When the tree has exhausted itself or been attacked by too many bugs, bacteria, whatever—it dies and its cells slowly decay with the help of water, oxygen, and microorganisms.

This thumbnail science lesson is interesting because by being rustic we insinuate ourselves into the very processes of life and afterlife. We jump right in with those trees and start to boogie—influencing, altering, elaborating what they do until the trees crumble to dust.

To put this another way, if you want your weekend rustic project to last, you have to interrupt the natural processes of wood decay. You have to dry the wood, either before or after you build with it, and keep the wood out of contact with the microorganisms that will help it decay.

ABOVE: Rustic arbor by Tom Holmes

LEFT: Bentwood chair by Andrew Gardner; see page 94 for instructions

BELOW: Outdoor rustic grouping by Daniel Mack

SELECTING YOUR MATERIALS

Even if you have access to a hundred acres, chances are you'll be limited to a few, maybe a half dozen, species of wood that are in the sizes you either want or can manage.

I suggest first seeing what is available to you. Then think, dream, and doodle with this specific wood in mind and see what happens. If it's a fast-growing pliant wood, such as willow, alder, or certain shrubs, you might think bentwood work—nails and hammers and curves. If the wood is small saplings, such as maple, hickory, or beech, you might think tables, ladders, bookcases, or a chair. Squint and see what your other eye sees when it imagines that tree disguised as something in your house.

Be guided, too, by what you need. What does your spouse need? What about the kids? Your mother?

Your approach to materials depends on the rest of your life. No two people see the trees, the woods, the materials, in the same way. In fact, no two people see a 2x4 in the same way.

Author's shop with wood stored on shelves

ABOVE: Rustic gate in Ausable, New York

RIGHT: Father and son show results from a week-long workshop

FAR RIGHT AND ON PAGE 30: Paintings by Suzanne Halligan

♥ Summer chair ♥

A FEW TIPS, WARNINGS, AND GUIDELINES ABOUT CUTTING MATERIALS

You only need a few things:

Bow saw or folding camp saw

Tape measure

Clippers

Rope and bailing twine

Sharp knife

Drinking water and fruit

First-aid kit

Do the clean up in the woods.

There is a certain drama to hauling a full tree out of the woods. But it will have to be trimmed up somewhere and cleaned up. Do it in the woods. Clip off leaves and small branches. I always size the wood in the woods as small as I dare. Usually, I cut and bundle wood in four- or five-foot lengths right in the woods. It's easier to move and move again and again. (And the shorter the length, the faster it dries.) With one-inch stock for rungs, I cut it in 24-inch lengths.

Pace yourself.

Remember, for every tree you cut there is about another half an hour of clipping, sizing, moving, bundling, loading. You have to drive home, unload, and store the cut wood in a dry airy place. The cutting is the easy part. I often don't get all the materials I need on the first trip or even the second. Remember, "rustic" is as much about altered ways and times of working as it is about odd furniture.

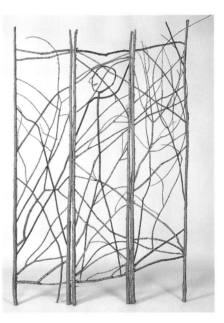

ABOVE: Gabriel Casey and one of his chairs

LEFT: Screen by Tor Faegre

BELOW: Unloading wood at a workshop

Deep forest trees are good.

They have had to survive in close, fierce proximity with their cousins. This has made them strong and dense with tight growth rings. This means you can get a lot of strength from a seemingly small diameter tree.

Twisted is not always better.

One of the first delights of rustic work is finding odd trees: big open ulcers, burls, vine twists, knot-like curves...WOW! But watch out...I still own most of the ones I cut in the early 1980s. Some are so unusual, they defy furniture. Some are just unusual enough that they call too much attention to themselves in a piece of furniture. Instead of "My, what a nice chair," all you hear is "What a twisted piece of wood!" It's nice to have a few pieces—they keep you humble.

"misproportions of Grandeur"

Impressions of a Daniel Mack Chair.

Go for the normal pieces.

The special quality to rustic work is the silk purse from the sow's ear...over and over; "Oh my, something so beautiful from materials so common!" Your job as a Rustic Warrior is to transform the plain into the special, the regular into the charmed—to illuminate the magic tucked into the regular. So the materials you want are the simple little trees. And then you invest your time and your sense of proportion in the making of some object you or part of your clan wants.

It helps to see what you have.

Unless you are blessed with a remarkable memory, you have to be able to see what wood you have. Look at pictures of how other rustics keep their wood. Last year I thought plastic garbage pails would do it. Then I tried plywood bins, then 2x4 racks, then metal shelves tipped back. I'm heading into year 20 of the always-less-than-perfect storage solution du jour. Really, my all-time favorite is to just lean everything against the wall!

Sometimes you don't need more materials.

Once in a while I just build from what I already own...no trip to the woods...JUST SAY NO to the Woods. And if I'm lucky, I get a little, tiny corner of space returned to me for some other use.

If you like the look of peeled wood, be patient.

You have to cut the trees just after they put out leaves if you want to peel off the bark. There are about six weeks when it is very easy to peel the bark off in long strips; after that it's inch by inch, and it looks all knicked up.

ABOVE: Andrew Gardner's green wood table uses the natural strength of tree forks.

BELOW: Large bins are perfect for storing wood.

TECHNIQUES

There is a collection of techniques used to handle wood in a rustic manner. None of these is very unusual, and all have been adapted from other forms of woodworking and craft. They fall into several overlapping categories, covering cutting, collecting, storing, constructing, and finishing.

CUTTING

Integral to this topic are two questions: Where can I get wood? What's the best time of year to cut?

Cut-Your-Own Wood

It's best to cut trees in the winter when the sap is down and the trees are least swollen. This means that when the cut pieces finally dry, there is less water to let off and less chance of the bark drying in a different way from the wood itself or blistering off. In addition, winter cutting minimizes the chances of active bugs and microorganisms.

However, life is not always fair, and it may not be possible to cut in the winter. I have cut every month of the year due to deadline, opportunity, wind storm, or some other contingency. Sometimes the wood has blistered as it has dried; other times it's been fine. This is all part of the magic of rustic; so don't let this "winter-cut" wisdom keep you from building.

I cut with a small folding saw. At the moment I like the Fiskars model. I have used bow saws and chain saws. All of these tools get the work done—some slower, some faster. Faster is not necessarily better. With the slowness of the bow saw comes some heat—and time to think about each cut and about where these wonderful pieces of tree might end up. A chain saw can deafen us to such thoughts. It usually demands attention like a two year old. It needs gas, oil, sharpening, coaxing, and it whines too much. It outrages us when it refuses to work. Our thoughts about the trees get lost.

The process of making a piece of rustic furniture literally starts in the woods: which tree, what diameter, and into what lengths is the tree to be cut for moving and storage. Decisions made then and there really shape the chair in a way no one piece of lumber can shape a piece of cabinetry.

Find-Your-Own Wood

Road crews are always trimming, tree services are always servicing, neighbors are always pruning, developers are always "clearing," town dumps always have brush piles. I will pay one dollar to anyone who can't find—within two miles of where he lives—wood to build with. I was able to find wood even when I lived in Manhattan! If you try to claim the one dollar prize, and I come to your town and find wood, you have to pay me TWO DOLLARS!

Buy-Your-Own Wood

In the last few years, several small mom-and-pop businesses have appeared that will sell you small amounts of kiln-dried saplings. A few are listed in the Resources section on page 108. In addition, you can call a local sawmill and ask about loggers who might cut you some smaller materials.

ABOVE: Driftwood pileup on a beach in British Columbia. PHOTO BY JACQUES GARANT

BELOW: Rustic fence at Olana, Hudson, New York

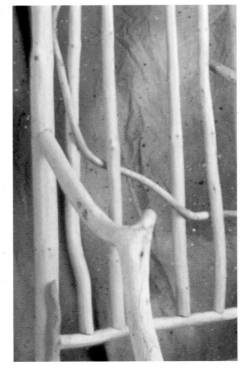

But Which Woods Are The Best?

The best wood for rustic work is *arbor availabilis*. Before you go to the tree guide, that means any wood you can get your hands on. Available Wood is very good wood because it lets you start making rustic furniture right away. Rustic work is local work, regionally inspired work. Get local woods and work with them. Soon you will become the local expert, not on which "woods are best," but on what all the different local woods are "best for." Remember, "rustic" is an attitude, not just a technical aptitude. This attitude is fundamentally different from the prevailing attitude of what constitutes "best," "efficient," or "productive." Rustic has much more to do with discovery, adventure, a lull, intuition, a hunch.

Peeled Wood

You can peel wood all year long, but for most of the year, the bark comes off in tiny little chunks that look like anchovies, and the wood itself ends up looking like a leftover at a beaver buffet. Easy peeling happens with a butter knife and comes off in very long, slurpy strips. To achieve that creamy smooth, no-tool-marks look, there is definitely a best time of year to peel wood. That's when the tree has just leafed out, and the juices are up and going, and before the heat of the summer thunks in. Where I live in lower New York state that time ranges between late May and mid-July. In Maine one summer, I was still peeling maple in August. Again, just keep trying. You'll find out to the day when it's "best" for you. I have been weaving seats this season with the long peelings from hickory that I stripped in June and early July.

I have used a pressure washer both at home and at the local car wash to remove the bark from trees. It makes for an odd afternoon. Some rustic makers wash the hand-peeled wood to get the dirt and sugars off the surface, and then they seal the ends with a wax or urethane. I do not. I just use the natural staining as part of the "look."

RIGHT: Detail of chair by Tim Dibble showing peeled pine and bittersweet.

DRYING TECHNIQUES

Dry wood is better than wet wood; it doesn't shrink, move, or check. Saplings, one to two inches in diameter, dry in a warm airy place in about two to four months. They are dry when they clack when you knock them together. The shorter you size the wood, the faster it dries.

There are several approaches available for drying wood. You can let wood sit in a dry, well-ventilated location; that might dry the wood in six months to two years. You can buy a kiln or build a kiln and dry a 4 x 4 x 16-foot load in a month. There are dehumidification kilns available for under $2,000. Many of the woodworking and boatbuilding magazines have featured articles about how to make your own. Kiln suppliers are listed in the Resources section on page 109. I have never used a kiln, but other rustics do. A kiln is good insurance against bugs hiding out in your wood, and a kiln is a good place to store wood for a while.

You can buy dry wood from suppliers (see Resources). You can choose a form of construction that doesn't really depend on dry wood, such as Andy Gardner's bentwood chair in the Festival section on page 94.

BELOW: Nick Parker's hazel and willow storage in Devon, England

What About Bugs?

There is a good chance that wood that has spent time on the forest floor or in your friend's woodpile has been visited by insects, fungus, and mildew. Look at the wood carefully before you decide to collect it for rustic work. If bugs are living in the wood, you may be bringing home more than the rungs for a chair.

The most damaging insects are the three kinds of wood-boring beetles—lyctids, anobids, and bostrichids. They are attracted to the starch in sapwood and are hard to discourage. To persuade beetles to relocate, I've injected turpentine into their holes, and I've heated the wood with a heat

ABOVE: Rustic gate by Daniel Mack, designed by Adele Mitchell

BELOW: Same gate installed

gun or heat lamp until the beetles leave. The best approach is to leave behind any wood that has obvious holes made by insects. When you get home, if you discover any wood with stowaway beetles, throw it out. Insects are less likely to inhabit driftwood, but you may find mildew and fungus on this type of wood; try stabilizing the wood with heat.

STORAGE

You can never be rich enough or have enough space to store sticks. That's a venerable truth. So make sure that whatever space you do have is dry and airy. That probably rules out a place behind the garage under a tarp, and it probably rules out the basement in the summer. It probably does make you think of the rafters in the garage, and maybe of building a rope-like scaffolding in your living room.

Wherever you store the wood, try to cut your wood into manageable lengths (48 inches or less). You will be appalled at how many times you have to move the same bundles of wood until you actually get to use them. And the shorter the lengths, the faster the wood dries.

RUSTIC JOINERY

Rustic Workshop 101: Joinery Techniques
(BRIEF SUMMARY): First you think and then you think some more. Then you cut. You mark. You drill. You whittle. You fit the pieces together. Then you look some more. Finally you tweak and glue.

That really is the whole picture. What varies is how you choose to join the pieces. There are several methods, ranging from a hammer and nail to the more challenging, but still fairly simple, mortise and tenon.

Before I review these traditional techniques, I would like to offer some alternatives. If rustic work is seen as a branch of woodworking, then the dominant woodworking tools and techniques would seem to be most sensible. But if you are making something rustic, which actually refers to life outside the dominant traditions—something "other"—then there is a world of techniques all competing for the attention of the Weekend Rustic.

For example, rustic fencing uses several forms of joinery techniques that can be applied to other forms of rustic work. The combination of pressure, weaving, and interlacing of branch material is a very effective and simple form of joinery. Sometimes, when you find a beautiful rustic stump or a piece of driftwood or a few beach stones, the most ancient form of joinery, Gravity, works best. Simply put the objects down and watch how they stay there. Walls and split rail fences are made this way.

There are other techniques even more fanciful. I have seen pieces of small rustic chairs joined with yarn, hot wax, hot glue, and Velcro. If you are a rustic inventor and not just a rustic drone, then there are no weird joints, just weird people. These rustic makers are experimenting with the conventional sense of time; they are not impressed with making something that seems immortal. They are joining a sense of humor and play and a message of the fleetingness of life into their work.

Gravity...
JOINERY ALMOST WITHOUT TOOLS

My favorite form of joinery is gravity, that free, always available, easily reversible form of keeping something on top of something else by just putting it there. One very quick project is to find a pleasant natural form and put it where you can see it...a piece of driftwood in the back yard or a small rock placed on a table or shelf. See how the object stays where you put it! Welcome to the rustic world!

I guess most of you are pretty experienced with gravity, which sometimes leads to another form of joinery: levity.

Stone arrangement by Christopher Owen, Block Island, Rhode Island

Levity is buoyancy, lightness, and wonder. As writer Robert Sardello wonders: How did the apple get up in the tree before Newton observed it in order to discover gravity? Levity got the apple UP.

By your choice of putting something someplace, you've created or "built" the opportunity for some interesting juxtaposition, for something provocative and perhaps beautiful. You've joined your sense of beauty, humor, and mystery with the experience of others. There is a natural levity to rustic work which is often called whimsy.

Conventional Construction with Nails and Screws

Mechanical techniques and devices are fine for getting two pieces of wood to stay together for a long while. All you need to do is position the pieces of tree where you want them, and put a nail into that spot, or a screw or lag screw, or a bolt. You can also use a wooden peg or dowel. It helps to predrill the top piece of wood with a bit that is slightly larger than the screw or nail, and predrill the bottom piece of wood with a bit that is slightly smaller than the screw or nail; the head of the screw or nail squeezes the first piece of wood tightly against the second. These joints are usually face joints where one piece of wood overlaps and crosses another. The appeal of this method is the quickness and relative simplicity of the tools and skills involved. The main drawback is the appearance of all those cut ends of wood blinking out from the finished piece. Another drawback is that you have to add diagonal pieces to prevent racking, pivoting, or hinging—the professional terms for wiggling.

A drawback of using nails is that they are hard to remove if you want to rearrange pieces of wood.

Nails are the fastest and crudest form of this type of joinery. Nails go into the wood and resist coming out, so you probably only have one chance to decide which way you like things put together. Laura Spector (page 90) puts her nails in with a heavy-duty, air-driven nailer. Andy Gardner uses a hammer (page 95).

A selection of nails and screws used in rustic work

("I see you used nails," says the Gremlin to the Rustic. "Yeah, so what!" says the Rustic.) I use mechanical joints for certain table designs and I think they are appropriate. The appearance of very small-headed trim screws has helped make the evidence of the mechanical joint less evident. But even if these nails or screws are very evident, there is an honesty in building and using ordinary supplies that is important in rustic work.

Author using an electric drill to drive screws

The Rustic Principle of Reversibility

Mechanical joints—screws, bolts, braces, and brackets, but NOT nails—move the job right along and can often be reversed or changed if the results need changing. Remember, rustic work is interactive design: one never really knows how a project is going to turn out until it's done.

Other mechanical joints include rope for lashing, and wire for lacing and sewing. In this application, the rustic is again not thinking like a woodworker, but as a sailor, seamstress, tailor, cook, cobbler, farmer, tinker. We all have old tradespeople buried in our DNA. There are "old ways" just waiting to be invited to the Rustic Workshop.

MORTISE AND TENON JOINERY

The prevailing construction technique in rustic work is the mortise and tenon—that's the old peg-in-the-hole, time-honored approach. The joinery is strong and makes the piece look like "real" furniture. It also takes a while to do. Put very simply, for most rustic work, a round peg is made on the end of one tree part, and this part fits snugly and deeply into an identically sized hole in the other tree part. Make sure to use very dry wood for your tenon (or peg). If a wet tenon shrinks as it dries in the hole, the joint may wobble.

Ways of Making Holes

The simplest way to make a hole is to use an electric drill with a sharp bit that puts the hole right where you want it. This means that the tip of the bit has to bite into the knurly, round face of the tree part and cut an accurate hole. For this job there are several different bits you can use.

Brad point bits have one sharp little toothy tang that keeps the bit from drifting. Sometimes these bits, also referred to as Bullet Bits or Irwin Bits, are available in hardware stores. They are also available in many of the catalogs listed in the tools sections of Resources (page 109).

Spade bits are big flat bits with a long fang to keep themselves in place. I like these bits, but they are very hungry for wood and will eat right through a small piece of wood. So use them on big wood, over 1¼ inches in diameter. Under that diameter, use brad point bits. Irwin Speedbore is a reliable brand. These bits are good for rustic work requiring holes from ⅝ inch to 1½ inches in diameter.

Big bits and extra long bits are available in some hardware stores, as well as in building-supply centers and plumbing and electrical-supply outlets. These may be needed for making 2-inch diameter holes for beds and big benches; the long bits may be needed for lamps or other unusual projects.

These bits fit in any of the electric drills on the market. I have a few different drills and prefer the cordless ones if I have enough extra batteries available.

LEFT TO RIGHT: Spade bit, brad point bit

Take Your Choice:

HAND AND POWER TOOLS FOR CUTTING TENONS

There are several ways to cut tenons or pegs for rustic furniture. There are many hand tools available that the causal maker can learn to use pretty quickly. There are a few ways to make these tenons with power tools, as well.

HAND TOOLS

A selection of hand tools for cutting tenons, LEFT TO RIGHT: Hatchet, pocket knife, brace operated hollow-auger and spoke pointer, and the Veritas tenon cutter

This is a quick and crude way to get a stick shaped down to fit in a hole.

Whittling gives you much more control… and calluses. Sometimes people start with the hatchet and finish up with the knife.

This recent tool, the Veritas tenon cutter, is really just a knife blade mounted in a solid wood block. When properly adjusted, it can quickly cut an accurate tenon.

POWER TOOLS

Several power tools for cutting tenons, CLOCKWISE FROM UPPER LEFT: DeWalt 18v cordless drill, heads for a stationary industrial tenon machine, Veritas tenon cutters, hole saws, spur cutters

Veritas tenon cutter for a drill. This cutter tapers the wood as it cuts and often a pre-tapering is not needed. It puts a curved shoulder on the tenon which is very obvious. There is a level built in to help keep the tenon straight on the wood.

Spur cutters fit only a ⅜" drill or a drill press, leaving a collar to be trimmed off. To start, the wood has to be tapered with a grinder, rasp, or spoke pointer.

Ways of Making Tenons

The better the fit, the stronger the joint. So there is quite a bit of care required to make a good tenon.

Whittling is a time-honored method: it's just very careful hatchet work. You use a sharp knife to whittle an almost perfect cylinder on the end of the stick. This needs to be done so well that the pieces actually squeak when you fit them together. If you succeed, you will feel proud and amazed, and then you will spend the next 20 minutes looking at the blisters on your right hand! I spent the first three years of building staring at these blisters which quickly turned into calluses.

Rasping is a folk approach to tenon-making. Here, a piece of wood, held in a vise, is filed away with a rasp or shurform tool, and made to fit the hole. People who don't like knives and don't want to use electric cutters are "raspers." It works.

Antique Tools

There is a pair of tools, the spoke pointer and the hollow auger, that used to be the Fred Astaire and Ginger Rogers of rustic work—lovely, traditional, the reference for all else. They were brace-operated. They are now somewhat difficult to find. If you find them, they will have to be adjusted and the small blades sharpened frequently. But they work. The spoke pointer, like a big pencil sharpener, tapers the wood to a point small enough to fit into the hollow auger, which is a two-edged cutter that makes perfect tenons of various diameters. Refer to the list of antique tool dealers in Resources (page 109) to find these tools.

Selection of tenon making tools and their product, LEFT TO RIGHT: pocket knife for whittling; Veritas tenon cutter for brace; spur cutter for drill.

Veritas tenon cutters have revolutionized the rustic world. Sculptor and arts teacher, Paul Ruhlmann, saw the antique hollow auger and spoke pointer at a workshop I taught in the early 1990s. He saw how fussy the old tools were—and they are hard to find. But he also observed what a great job the cutters did. So he developed two different types. One fits into a brace and works quietly; the other fits into a ⅜-inch electric drill and sounds like a piglet. They both cut accurate, handsome pegs. And they are affordable.

Hole saws, spur-headed tenon cutters, and lathes can all be used to make tenons. I suggest that a new weekend rustic builder use a knife, or the Veritas cutters, or invent some personal way to accomplish this task.

Another way to make a mortise and tenon joint is to use a traditional woodworking blind-dowel joint. For rustic work, you will need to put a hole in both tree parts to be joined; then you insert and glue a length of purchased dowel between the two members. (see Mark Nimal's chairs in the Rustic Festival section, page 92.)

Cutting Square Mortises and Tenons

Porter used through tenons on this cherry bed.

Robbie Porter, of Adamant, Vermont, applies fine woodworking skills to his rustic work. For the large beds he builds, he carefully cuts square mortises and tenons on all his joints. The great advantage of this square joint is the locked fit once the piece is together. The drawback is the absolute exactness needed to make it all work. Its success is a testimony to both the hand and the eye of a rustic craftsman.

Here Porter is using a Japanese saw to cut a square tenon from osage orange.

Each piece of this Mississippi driftwood headboard is laid out in position and marked.

LEFT AND RIGHT: Partially assembled headboard made from butternut

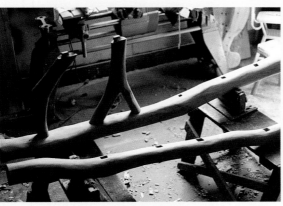

DESIGN TECHNIQUES (OR) WHAT SHOULD I MAKE?

One very workable approach to get you started is to find a nice chair, table, or bookcase, and copy it using sticks for parts. Don't worry—no intellectual property lawyers will come after you. And you will be amazed at how the sticks will change even the simplest design of a table, bench, or chair. There is an easy design approach described in the Panel Section on page 59, and great-looking rustic work throughout the book to inspire you.

CONSTRUCTION TECHNIQUES: WHAT GLUE DO YOU USE?

After you've made the holes and squeaked the near-perfect tenons into them, you must take it all apart and glue it. You must. Carefully wipe regular yellow carpenter's glue on all faces of the wood and then fit the pieces back together. I often mark each piece and its position with chalk so it ends up looking like it first did. It's very important that you clamp or strap the glued pieces together for the first four to six hours after you glue them. Most carpenter's glues set under pressure. Bar clamps and vise clamps are okay, but web clamps or strap clamps are best for conforming to the usually odd shapes of rustic work. There are several new glues on the market that set chemically, but I haven't used them.

FINISHING: WHAT DO YOU DO AFTER IT'S DONE?

After the frame is assembled, there is still a task ahead to get the piece "finished" so it looks like more than a bunch of tree parts glued together. This finishing is a process of softening and aging the look of the piece. Some rustic woods resist finishing. Golden birch is "finished" almost as soon as you have decided to use it; so is cherry and white birch—although all of these can handle a coat of tung oil varnish to make them look a little less "new."

Finishes for Bark

Finishing a rustic piece with a 1:1 mixture of boiled linseed oil and turpentine or mineral spirits changes the color of the wood. A finish of this type keeps the energy of the piece going: it's unexpected; the wood still looks like a tree and feels so smooth. This recipe works well for all types of wood with bark, except cherry and birch, which don't absorb liquids very well.

Here's what you do:

1. Saw or grind any branch scars or rough bark areas that are too sharp or abrasive.

2. Fine sand these areas only with a finer paper until you get them as smooth as desired.

3. With a fine paper (220 or 150) or a sanding sponge, wipe down the rest of the piece, emphasizing areas of possible wear with a little extra sanding. Don't dig in too much. The purpose is to clean off dirt, small burrs, and open the surface of the bark so the oil mixture can be absorbed easily.

4. Put on neoprene gloves and wipe the mixture onto the wood.

5. After a day or two repeat the oil application and let the wood dry thoroughly.

6. Wipe down the wood with a cloth.

7. Apply a wax with 0000 steel wool; then buff.

ABOVE: Bench by
Barry Gregson

RIGHT: Entry table
of peeled wood,
Daniel Mack

BELOW: Red cedar
immediately
changes color
when white
vinegar is applied
with steel wool.

For maple, hickory, and beech, I sand with 220-grit paper and then apply several coats of boiled linseed oil, cut with mineral spirits (50/50). Then I wax over that and buff.

Staining rustic work is something I do only when asked. Sometimes the client wants a very consistent color in the finished piece. In that case, I lightly sand the bark, stain the piece with a walnut stain, finish with a linseed oil and mineral spirit mix, and then wax and buff.

With peeled woods, I apply an oil-base urethane, followed by a clear butcher's wax applied with 0000 steel wool; then I buff.

To preserve driftwood's weathered look, but to make it feel smooth, I lightly sand it with a 220-grit paper to remove the dirt and burrs. Then, just to harden the surface, I apply a coat of acrylic urethane, diluted with water 50/50. Lastly, I wax over that using 0000 steel wool. Then I buff the wood.

Other Ways to Finish Wood

An oil finish makes the wood look like old leather. Basically, the finish I like best is one that makes the wood look old. Here are two other techniques I have been using in the last few years for finishing and aging raw wood.

White vinegar, when applied with steel wool, reacts with certain woods to turn them a darker color—from a silver toning on maple to jet black on cedar. I'm still experimenting with the number of applications, the use of the sun, and various woods. But on this fresh red cedar, I was able to speed up the aging process so that the wood looked the way cut cedar would if left outside for a year or so. This gave the newly finished piece a consistency of tone.

Lye, usually a tablespoon to a quart of warm water, wiped on cherry wood, darkens and deepens the color to what it would be after years of exposure to the light.

For both of these treatments, I wear neoprene gloves and safety goggles, and I try to work outside the shop. Then I apply a polyurethane or oil finish, over the raw wood treatment, and finish with a wax applied with 0000 steel wool.

Please notice that these treatments give an inconsistent result; that is, there are darker parts and lighter parts. This is not a negative for me: the effect reflects the subtle inconsistencies of all rustic materials. I prefer the inconsistency. There is a homemade quality to them or to the way I do them that I like. Stains from cans are so predictable and dull compared to the vibrancy of some of these old-time finishing techniques. Remember, they work on raw, unfinished wood.

SEATING TECHNIQUES

Seating is the last frontier of rustic work. Everybody's sense of what's "right" is a bit different. I won't attempt to convince you that my current attraction to the upholstered seat is more or less "correct." There are several ways to work.

The wooden rustic seat is very traditional. Planks of wood are screwed or nailed or pegged onto the frame. These pieces might be small, full-round branches, splits of a small log that are band sawed or sanded and grinded out, or worked on a shaving horse with a drawknife. A wooden seat of this type keeps the country-tree-rustic feel of the chair frame going.

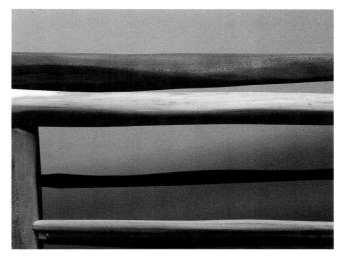

ABOVE: The effect is dramatic when lye is wiped on cherry.

BELOW: Wooden seats complement these simple but elegant antique stick chairs.

RIGHT: An early stick chair by Daniel Mack, featuring a woven seat
PHOTO BY BOBBY HANSSON

BELOW: A pair of Daniel Mack's chairs with upholstered seat cushions

Woven seats are often the most comfortable. Various materials are interwoven onto the chair frame. Shaker tapes have been popular and are available, with instructions, from a variety of places listed in Resources on page 109. But first, I suggest you go to a local upholstery shop to look for belting or cording or even materials that can be folded into strips and woven. Craft-supply stores carry a wide variety of natural and manufactured materials suitable for weaving. Large building-supply stores carry a variety of ropes, strings, and other materials that can be drafted into use as seating. Approach these places with the same sense of adventure you bring to the woods. Directions for the weaving can be found at craft shops or in the books listed in the Resources section.

Upholstered seats are my favorite. With these, I cut a piece of ⅝-inch plywood to fit the seat frame of the chair. I drill four holes in the center area of the seat board to let air in and out. Then I take the board to my local upholsterer with a fabric I have selected, and have it professionally covered as a tight seat, or a seat with welting, or any of the options offered. Then I screw the finished seat into the frame from beneath, through a hole I have predrilled, so that the screw head is countersunk.

I tried upholstery myself and quickly learned that my rustic upholstery looks cheesy. Other rustics, like Michelle Ellsworth (see page 87 in the Rustic Festival section), seem to have a greater talent for doing this themselves.

Proximity and Pressure:

TOOLS REQUIRED

Related to gravity is proximity and pressure; things get put next to each other in such a way as to stay. Weaving is the most common way of achieving this, and there are rustic versions of plaiting and weaving. For instance, in England there is a long tradition of woven hurdle fence making and wattle fence building which is making its way to the United States. I recently saw an example of this style in the gardens just outside the Cathedral of Notre Dame in Paris.

One technique of woven fences requires sturdy uprights, either wood or metal (such as #7 rebar), driven 12 inches into the ground about every 18 inches for small fences, and every 24 inches for larger fences. Then you collect a supply of very fresh supple wood and weave it from each end into the center. Clip or saw off any stray ends. It's okay if one of the weavers cracks; it's easy to weave back around it.

TOP OF PAGE: Woven fence outside the Cathedral of Notre Dame in Paris

CENTER: Woven fence being built in author's garden. Rebar has been driven into holes prepared with a long auger drill attachement, then wood is woven through these uprights.

BOTTOM: Completed fence

Insider Tips from a Rustic Maker

WEST COAST BUILDER GORDON GRABE SENT ALONG A FEW OF HIS TIME-TESTED METHODS OF WORKING WITH NATURAL WOOD.

Vinegar and Iron Wood Stain

I use a mixture of vinegar and steel wool to forcibly age the ends of branches and bare wood.

> **THE FORMULA: 1 gallon of vinegar, 2 washed pads of steel wool.**

Stuff the steel wool pads down the neck of a jug and cover the jug opening with cloth, securing with a string or rubber band around the neck. **IMPORTANT NOTE: DO NOT SEAL JUG WITH A SCREW CAP; A CHEMICAL REACTION IS TAKING PLACE AND THE JUG WILL EXPLODE!**

This formula works best with woods containing tannic acid. Most hardwoods and softwoods, such as pine, have tannic acid. One of the exceptions is oleander, which contains oxalic acid; this acid will actually bleach out the effects of the vinegar and iron natural wood stain. This is true for citric acid or fabric bleach, as well. A solution of water and potassium permanganate or a solution of water and baking soda also reacts with tannic acid, each giving a different color of stains.

I apply the vinegar/iron stain with a brush. The stain will darken with age; the concentration of the solution and the moisture in the air cause the wood to darken. Making tests with different concentrations over a period of a month or so will give you a good gauge as to what the properties of your formula should be. **Tip:** Low concentrations are the best way to start. I've been surprised as to how long-acting and powerful this stain is. **Suggestion:** Try 1 cup of water to 1 tablespoon of a one-week-old vinegar and steel wool solution. You may want to strain the steel wool out of the jug and label the jug, using it to mix from as you need it.

These chemicals have been used for centuries and are discussed in a lot of books on woodworking, but their application in the rustic craft is not much talked about. There seems to be a gap in old traditional woodworking techniques and the rustic furniture techniques. It seems like there has been little communication between the two woodworking traditions.

Peeling Wood

Be careful using pressure washers to peel bark: they'll blow the bark away on old dried branches, and, on new branches, they can blow right down to the wood and beyond, if you're not careful.

The "no pressure wash" that I use the most is to soak branches in water, alternating with periods of drying, over a period of two months. I have a creek out back, and, when it's running, I soak a tied bundle of branches. It's just like making your own driftwood.

Curing Branches

If you put wax on the ends of your cut branches, it will prevent them from cracking and splitting.

Finishes

For bare wood indoor furniture I use a paste wax only. If I leave the bark on, I use a clear, waterborne, satin polyurethane varnish. Varnishing bark toughens the loose parts of the bark. For outdoor furniture I use varnish, linseed oil, and turpentine mixed equal parts.

Ornamentals

I have made furniture using mulberry, oleander, japanese plum, hollywood juniper, persimmon, twisted willow, eucalyptus, rose cane, English walnut, and fig. We have a moderate climate out here in California where just about anything grows. I find that using ornamentals adds more choices to the rustic furniture maker's palette. One of my favorite pieces is a rose cane basket with a fig branch handle. It's for carrying roses in from the garden!

ABOVE: Rustic maker
Jerry Farrell's
workshop

RIGHT: Student at a
rustic workshop using
a tenon cutter

BELOW: An assortment
of tools used by rustic
makers

TOOLS

**Four rustic tools you already have:
the Body, the Eye, Time, and the Hand.**

Normal woodworking tools are made for
handling lumber, a distant cousin—the
American Cheese—of trees. These tools are
meant to make things straight and flat. There
is almost nothing like that in the woods. The
woods are bumpy, curved, sinuous, and
arching. The Woods reflect perfectly the
crooked ways of life. It's difficult, sometimes
unpleasant, to be reminded of this, so it's
tempting to dismiss the woods and the Rustic
Furniture which reflects it, as unrefined,
clumsy, and oafish.

Rustic woodworking offers a doorway into
another world of making where you must
discover and confront your own sense of
design and proportion and invoke the beautiful in your own way. It's an opportunity for a
meandering, impromptu encounter where all
of several choices might work.

The key tool is the Body. It provides the
essential frame of reference—the viewpoint
on the world and the physical connection to
gesture, the human animation through which
we convey unspoken messages to our fellows.
Our body and the bodies of others are a rich
grammar of emotion and action. The gesture
of the arm, the foot, the extended hand, the
arched back, the tilted head, the open
chest...body language is a fundamental part
of all furniture and especially rustic furniture. When these gestures are discovered and
selected from the trees, they become doubly
powerful as the message of furniture because,
along with the gesture intended by the
furniture maker, is the residual shape, texture, and history of the tree itself.

The Eye estimates. It admires, sizes up, approves, squints, winces at the rights and wrongs of making work from trees; I believe we all have an aesthetic sense. It may not be highly practiced, but in every course I teach, the people who claim they have "no eye" for this work are the ones who become very choosy about branches of the right diameter, curve, or texture. With a little encouragement, their personal sense of beauty starts to emerge, and they begin to feel a special kind of authorship for their work.

Rustic woodworking requires an altered sense of Time. The rustic worker is linked to the rhythms of the seasons for cutting and drying wood, to the mysteries of various tree blights and insect attacks, and to the creative rhythm of making something without a pre-set design. Rustic woodworking is responsive woodworking: responsive to the seasons, the idiosyncrasies of individual trees, and the murkiness of the creative process. The moods of the maker are affected by time. I try to think about what's going on, what time of day it is… is this a good time to keep working? I try to pay attention to the less than loud voices that are always informing me about what's going on. Intuition and patience are a few of the key attitudes required in good making. All of this makes for less than a production-line schedule. It's hard to predict when certain rustic projects will get finished. In that way, rustic woodworking seems a bit out of control and gets talked about as a folk art or naïve furniture.

The Hand is the Proto-tool. It has strength and near-infinite motions to grasp, turn, angle, pose, position, twist, grab, and discard. Units of measurement are hand-based: the inch, a pinch, a handful, two-fingers. Remember, hands are not perfect; they are different sizes. Fingers have been cut, sliced, and healed oddly; fingers curl and stiffen. Strength comes and goes.

Other Tools—Extensions of the Hand

There are only really three kinds of invented tools needed for rustic work; they are all extensions of your hands. There is now a very rich selection of tools available, with great attention paid to balance, ergonomics, beauty, and even the fact that people other than 200-pound loggers might want to use a tool. You need:

1. Cutting and shaping tools, used for getting the wood into the sizes and forms you can use;

2. Drilling tools, for making the holes for pegs, tenons or nails and screws;

3. Assembly tools, for getting and keeping the work together.

CUTTING TOOLS

Not surprisingly, these include saws. I like the folding camping and pruning saws; they fit into your back pocket, and the blades have fast-cut double-set teeth. The new Fiskars model has a very comfortable black handle and a good blade locking system. Both the Coghlan's and Coleman folding camping saw work well also. These saws can also be used in the shop for bench work, but I like a bigger saw. The Jack Pro or the Stanley Shortcut are both short enough and rigid enough for good bench trimming.

I use several power saws. I have several chain saws—a few gas-powered ones (which I haven't used in years) for the woods, and a few of the smallest electric ones I can find, usually with a 10-inch bar. This one is very helpful for roughing various projects in and just outside the shop; it's small enough to still be an extension of my body, and it doesn't spit out all the exhaust of the gas models.

Some of rustic builder David Robinson's favorite tools

Student drilling a hole in a stick

Dirk Leach using a horizontal pneumatic drum sander

I have used a 10-inch miter saw or chop saw for the last ten tears as my primary shop saw. I now use a 12-inch DeWalt; it's comfortable and reliable, and the fence is big enough to wedge odd-shaped sticks against it. (But do see the accident log for a story about this tool.)

I have a circular saw and a newer 18-volt battery operated one that handles a lot of the simpler flat cutting jobs.

I have never owned a table saw, but I did have a 12-inch radial arm saw in one shop for about seven years. It was more than I needed and had the habit of dominating me every few weeks by spitting a stick through a window. I abandoned it when I left that shop.

I keep a few Japanese dozuki saws near my worktable, but the blades are generally too thin for the quirks of rustic work.

Other Cutting Tools

Clippers are very important to me. I have several different kinds, and more, if you add loppers into the category. Clippers/loppers let me cut up to 1-inch stock with just the squeeze of a hand. The kinds I use are rachet operated, made by American Standard or Fiskars.

SANDING-GRINDING

I consider sanding tools a variation of cutting tools: they remove stock.

The key tool here is a sander-grinder—not the disc that goes on the electric drill—but a tool of its own. It's faster than a drill-sanding attachment, and really lets me shape and sculpt the ends of sticks. Plus, it softens knots, branch scars, and swells.

I have lots of different sanders: belt sanders, palm sanders, random orbital sanders...they all get used sometimes. But I also like the 3M palm-size sanding sponges that come with different grits on opposite sides. These sponges let you respond gently to the contours of rustic work in a way a power sanding device cannot.

DRILLING TOOLS

I use an old Craftsman drill press from 1962 that I bought at a yard sale. It's simple and friendly. And I like the way it looks back at me; it has a nice face.

I must have a dozen other drills: old ¼-inch chrome-bodied ones from the '50s and '60s, as well as a good assortment of ones with cords and ones that are battery operated. It's essential to own a ½-inch drill; this means the opening on the chuck is big enough to take an attachment, such as a drill bit, which has a ½-inch diameter shank. This kind of drill is very powerful boring into green and dry wood, and will throw you around if you're not holding on very tight. Some come with an additional side handle. I may have three or four drills ready on any one building project. Each will have a different drill bit or screwdriver head or chamfering bit.

Take Care!

A LOG OF SHOP MISHAPS THAT HAVE HAPPENED TO RUSTIC MAKERS...NO NAMES, JUST REAL ACCIDENTS...

Watch that Blade

"I was set back months. The ease of the chop saw fooled me into thinking it didn't require careful handling. I braced an especially curvy branch only with my hand and not against the back fence—my fingers didn't reach. The branch wiggled, caught the blade, and jerked the two-inch sapling up against the fence with my finger in between. This happened with such force that it took four months for me to finally regain the complete use of the finger. The nail turned black and fell off."

Climbing Trees

"My biggest accidents occur when I am out climbing trees. Last year I fell out of a big willow tree and landed on my back. I was okay, but I had some pretty painful ribs for a few months. I'm still climbing trees after almost 50 years. What a great life! In the shop, most of the danger occurs when I try to use tools for dimensional wood on round wood. This requires some unusual jigs, but I haven't had any real disasters."

The Hazards of Working with Vines

"I have to climb trees to collect vines for my work and I have fallen out of trees several times. Usually, I land in piles of leaves, but recently I hit a rock and broke my heel. (Every year I get a shot for poison ivy!) I use a nail gun to put my work together and have had a few accidents...once I nailed through my hand and another time into the muscle near my thumb."

Animals in the Shop

"An old woodworker and shop teacher told us young cubs that power tools are wild animals, and that they can't wait to ruff you up and take a bite out of you. An image of a black bear looms in my mind every time I approach a mindless power tool.

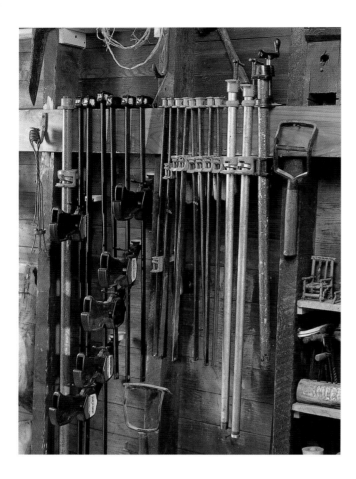

ABOVE: Bar clamps hanging in author's shop

RIGHT: Brent McGregor sandblasting a large tree stump

HOLDING TOOLS

I can still count all 10 of my fingers, thank you. That is due, in part, to how I hold tools.

There are several methods for holding tools. For example, when I use the drill press, I usually use V-blocks to hold stock. Sometimes I use a drill-press vise. Sometimes I use spring clamps or vise clamps to hold something together while I drill. I'll use pipe clamps to really pull a panel together, and I'm always using strap clamps or webclamps in my chairmaking. I have a few dollies around the shop to hold and move boxes. There are a few bench- mounted vises; the Workmate table is a good holding tool. I'm always grabbing for the vise grips, channel pliers, or needle-nose pliers.

TIPS ABOUT TOOLS AND STICKS

It's an unhappy relationship...what can I say? The toolmakers think flat and square when they design tools. Nature doesn't think—it's all this way and that...fluid-curvy. That's what we rustics are drawn to. So there has to be some extra thought given to using tools, especially power tools with natural forms.

Work down.

Get a worktable that you can rest your elbows on comfortably. This will allow you to have more control over the work and the tools. Work with your arm as close in to your body as possible. You'll have more coordination and be able to use all your strength. This is especially important for women; the right height worktable will give you maximum control on the tools and the work. You have the best chance to make work rather than tire yourself fighting the table. Try working at different height tables to see what I mean. I have three different height worktables for different kinds of projects, and I still find myself on my knees on the floor a lot.

Sting the wood.

Again, most tools are made for addressing flat lumber. For the round, erratically round, surfaces of rustic work, you need tools which bite in or sting the wood where you want to. The Speedbore bits have a long toothy tang and there are a lot of brad-pointed bits around—drill bits with a small sharp tooth in the center to keep the bit in place so it doesn't wander or jump.

Dress for the job.

I now wear gloves as much as possible: thin, tight leather "ranch-hand" gloves for handling material, latex gloves for some finishing, and neoprene gloves for work with bleach, lye, and other finishes.

I try to keep my shirttails tucked in…there are a lot of hungry spinning devices around.

Keep the air clean.

I have a three-part air filter in my 5400-cubic-foot shop, and recently I put in an air ionizer and ozonator. When I have to sand in the shop, I hook a vacuum up to a sanding tray.

Why Have Several of the Same Tool?

Some people believe that tools have their own lives. There is a mystery to tools. Sometimes some work and sometimes they are not cooperative. I understand that, so I have other ones available which may be more willing to work with me.

Tools, like children, pets, and other relationships, require time and attention for cleaning and care and admiration. Nonetheless, that does not guarantee peak performance all the time. It's best to have a few cousins available.

Finally, I have several places I like to keep tools. Some here, some there, some upstairs, some in the basement. Just think: what if an earthquake trapped me in the back of my shop and the only cordless drill was in the front of the shop?

Sometimes a new tool comes on the market, and it's so beautiful, and fast, and powerful. It's balanced so well. But my old tool still works fine.

This is why I have several of each tool.

Tool List

A LIST OF THE TOOLS AND SUPPLIES I USED IN MY SHOP LAST YEAR

Cutting	Folding handsaw	Shortcut or jacksaw	Circular DeWalt 18v cordless
	DeWalt 12-inch miter saw	Pruning clippers	Knives/chisels
	Fiskars loppers	Hitachi corded circular saw	Electric chain saw
	Surform rasps		
Drills	DeWalt 18v cordless	Extra batteries	Chargers
	DeWalt 12v cordless	Makita 7.2v cordless	Makita corded
	Drill press	1/2-inch Porter cable corded	
Drill Bits	Full set brad point	Large bits 1 1/2"	Speedbore bits
	Short / extra long bits		
Tenon Cutting	Lee Valley tenon cutters	Hole saws	Spoke pointer
Electric	Extension cord	Halogen clamp light	3-prong to 2-prong adaptor
	Webar		
Holding	Workmate table	Quick Grip clamps	Vises
	Needle nose pliers	Web clamps	Pipe clamps
	Tension clamps	C-clamps	Folding sawhorses
	Vise grips	Channel pliers	V-blocks
Other Tools	Hammer	Rubber mallet	Pliers
	Sawhorses	Grinder discs	Allen wrenches
	Tape measure	Random orbital sander/paper	Vacuum cleaner
	Hachet /adze	Sander / grinder	Compass
Supplies	Trim head screws	Extra heads #1 and #2	Decking screws
	String / rope	Finishing nails	Linseed oil
	Sandpaper	Sanding sponges	Carpenter's glue
	Polyurethane glue	Epoxy	Tacks / brads
	Duct tape	Masking tape	Rags
	Tarps	Flashlight	Broom
	Pens / pencils	Chalk	Extra driver heads
	Level	Chalk line	Framing square
Safety	Work gloves	Adhesive bandages	Peroxide
	Finger tape	Dust mask	Safety glasses

PROJECTS

Projects are wonderful things. They are the end result of a process of projecting yourself into the future. They are imaginings that can take on material presence. Or, they may remain merely projections.

What is a project? It's a creative exercise in order and harmony…a fundamental creative act that's as important to humans as air, food, and water. A project can last over a period of time, and its result may outlive its maker and take on quite new significance—as a family heirloom or part of a yard sale.

Projects also provide the maker with the opportunity to learn or relearn some things about time, and collect evidence of the fleeting and the invisible by looking and engaging in the visible. That means being aware of the importance of the thinking, talking, planning, and preparing that precedes a project…and the moving, sorting, and placing that post-dates the making of the item. The item is only part of the project.

BUILDING APPROACHES TO PROJECTS

In this section I start by explaining and illustrating the primary way I build rustic furniture by making simple ladders or panels and joining them together. For some of you this will be the "aha" you've been wanting. You'll see several kinds of furniture you can make with a simple ladder construction.

Secondly, I explain and illustrate how I make one particular form of furniture: a table. I show different construction approaches, some of which will be more appealing to you than others.

Thirdly, like a good magician, I disappear…or seem to. I invited eight weekend rustics to demonstrate how they make things. This gives you the chance to see other ways of thinking and working with natural-form materials. Along the way, I offer a number of asides that reflect my experience as a rustic builder and as a maker of things. For instance, I have a particular admiration of joinery using only gravity.

I would suggest reading through the three sections first. Then you can decide in what way you want to make projects and where to start. All the ways are fine.

Panels

MAKING PANELS

One orderly way to create rustic furniture is to make panels. I take four, five, six or more pieces of wood and combine them into frames, ladders, or panels; then I join them to form chairs, beds, tables, bookcases, room dividers, arbors, fences, gates, stools, etc. When you make panels, you are reducing and simplifying the number of pieces of wood you are working with—combining several pieces to make one panel. At the end, you have one piece of furniture. This approach has served me well in my 20 years of building.

The panel can be made by attaching the wood pieces with nails, screws, glue, rope, or rawhide. Some of these methods work better than others with particular materials and designs. Experiment to see what works best for what you are trying to make. The chart below offers a few suggestions.

MAKING A
SEVEN-FOOT
LADDER

*The ladder form is the basis of
the panel. It's made with two
vertical upright posts and several
horizontal rungs or stretchers,
and, if you like, a diagonal or two.*

What You Need

2 straight posts of 2- to 2½-inch
saplings, each about 84 inches long

6 rungs of 2-inch saplings,
each about 18 inches long

measuring tape

cutting tools

black marker

vise and vise clamps

chalk

tenon-cutting tools

drill with ¾-inch spade bit
or brad bit in a drill press

rubber mallet

hammer

finishing nails

What You Do

1. Cut the posts square on the
bottoms.

2. Hold the posts together so
they line up; then mark arrows
on the bottoms to help you
remember the lined-up position.

3. Lay out your posts so they will stay straight and in place. You can accomplish this with a vise and vise clamps.

4. Use chalk to mark each post from the bottom at 12 inches, 24 inches, 36 inches, 48 inches, 60 inches, and 72 inches. Put this mark along the imaginary line indicated "UP" by your arrow.

5. Drill a ¾-inch hole about 1 inch into each of the posts at the indicated marks. You can do this with a spade bit in a drill or a brad bit in a drill press.

6. Prepare tenons on the ends of each of your rungs. Make sure the tenons are 1-inch cylinders. You can whittle the tenons with a sharp knife, or use a mechanical tenon cutter or a power tenon cutter. (Refer to page 41 for information about cutting tenons.)

7. Assemble the ladder by fitting all the rungs into one post and then into the other. You may have to twist each rung until you find the best way to fit them all together.

8. Use a rubber mallet to get a secure fit.

9. Put a small finishing nail through the face of the ladder, into the tenon.

10. If the ladder racks or wiggles, you may want to add one or two 45-degree diagonal braces to steady it. Use scraps of 1-inch saplings for this purpose.

BASIC BOOKCASE

H*ere's some advice on building a bookcase using two tall ladders. The finished bookcase shown here is about 36 inches wide, 48 inches tall, and 12 inches deep. Once you've built this one, you'll have your own ideas about variations to make it taller, wider, or narrower, perhaps with deeper shelves or more decoration.*

What You Need

FOR THE TWO LADDERS

4 posts of 2-inch saplings, each 60 inches tall

4 rungs of 1-inch saplings, each 13 inches long

FOR THE TWO STRETCHERS

2 pieces cut from 1-inch saplings, each 36 inches long

measuring tape

cutting tools

Surform rasp

tenon-cutting tool

drill and assorted bits

rubber mallet

screwdriver

decking screws

What You Do

Building the Ladders and Frame

1. Make the two ladders, following the instructions on pages 59–60.

2. Now make the four stretchers.

3. Put ¾-inch tenons, 1 inch deep, on each end.

4. Drill holes into the face of each ladder post, measured up from the bottom at 11 inches and 47 inches.

5. Assemble the bookcase frame by putting all the rungs into one ladder, then fit the other on in place. Twist the stretchers until there is a snug fit and the frame sits squarely on the floor. Because of the variations in natural forms, you may choose to replace one or two of the 36-inch long stretchers with shorter or longer ones.

6. After this basic frame is acceptable, knock it apart; then glue the tenons into the mortises or cross nail each joint with a finishing nail.

Adding Shelves

This bookcase was designed for regular 1 x 12 lumber from your local building-supply outlet. You can choose pine or hardwoods or the composite shelving sold by many of these stores.

7. Measure the distance from the outside edges of the ladders that make up the sides of your bookcase. If you made it as I suggested, that distance should be about 36 inches.

8. Now cut your shelving about 2 inches longer than that measurement.

9. Measure the distance between the posts of your ladder; that might be about 11 inches. Your store-bought shelves are about 11½ inches, which means you'll have to take a little notch out of each corner of your 36-inch-long shelves to make them fit and look fitted. There are several ways to do this, using a hand-saw, jigsaw, or Surform rasp.

10. Put your shelves in place and straighten up the book-case, making sure it's not leaning too much in any one direction. If you're happy with what you see, fix the shelves in place with screws from the bottom side or the top side. You should predrill the wood first.

11. How does the bookcase look? Done? Congratulations!

12. Not quite done? Does it wiggle? Add a few curved braces. Does it look too square? Cut the front posts down to 1 inch above the shelf. Does it look too bare? Add a few decorative pieces on the back, front, or sides. Does it look too new? You can sand the edges of the boards, or you can sand the saplings a bit and put some linseed oil on the wood. If you want, you can paint the shelves. Does it still wiggle? You can brace the bookcase right to the wall when you find the perfect place for it.

FOUR-PANEL ROOM SCREEN

*T*his is one way to build a room screen or divider using a basic panel construction. The one shown here measures about 48 inches wide, 84 inches tall, and 12 inches deep. Depending on the materials you collect, yours might have only three panels, be wider or shorter, or have more or less embellishment.

What You Need

FOR THE FOUR LADDERS

8 posts of 2-inch saplings, each 84 inches tall

16 rungs of 1-inch saplings, each 22 inches long

measuring tape

cutting tools

tenon-cutting tool

drill and assorted bits

150-grit sandpaper or sanding sponge

mixture of 50/50 boiled linseed oil and mineral spirits

4 pairs of rawhide boot laces, 36 inches long

materials for decorating the screen

What You Do

Building the Ladders

1. Follow the instructions for building a ladder on pages 59–60, but omit the rungs at 36 and 48 inches.

2. Do you like the gray color of the wood? If so, skip ahead to step 5.

3. Do the ladders look too rough? If so, lightly sand the ladders with a 150-grit sandpaper or sanding sponge; then rub on a mixture of 50/50 boiled linseed oil and mineral spirits to darken the wood.

4. Do you want the wood to be lighter? Add water to white latex paint to get a 50/50 mix, and rub it on with a soft rag. Let the paint dry. Then lightly sand the wood and oil it as described in step 3.

Assembling the Screen

5. Lay a pair of ladders next to each other on the floor, about an inch apart.

6. Tie the pair together loosely with rawhide laces, just above the top rung and again just above the bottom rung. Repeat this procedure with the next pair of ladders. Last, join both pairs together, as shown in the photograph on page 63.

7. Stand the screen up and admire your work so far.

8. You have built a room divider with a hole in the middle of every panel. What do you want to do with it now? Here are a few suggestions: You can staple on sheets of translucent Japanese paper to create an oriental affect. Fabric tied to the panels in strategic places could look beautiful. You can weave leather over and under the rungs. How about gluing or nailing on delicate twigs and sprigs of berries? You can string beads or seashells onto string and tie them to the screen. These are just a few possibilities.

GARDEN ARBOR

There are so many ways you can build a beautiful arbor with basic ladders. Here's an arbor that is about 36 inches wide, 84 inches tall, and 18 inches deep. After you've made one arbor, you'll have many ideas for creating other ones using different materials and methods. Bernadette Scutaro and Sharon Kimmelman worked on this arbor.

What You Need

FOR THE TWO TALL LADDERS

4 posts of 2-inch saplings, each 108 inches tall

16 rungs of 1-inch saplings, each 18 inches long

FOR THE ONE SHORT LADDER

2 posts of 2-inch saplings, 60 inches tall

4 rungs of 1-inch saplings, 18 inches long

3-inch diameter PVC pipe, 60 inches long

cutting tools

tenon-cutting tools

drill and assorted bits

carpenter's glue

measuring tape

hole-digger or trowel

sand, gravel, or cement

decking screws

What You Do

1. Build the three ladders, following the instructions on page 59–60.

2. Cut the PVC pipe into four 14-inch-long pieces.

3. Measure the distance, center to center, between the bottoms of each of the ladders in your arbor. Let's say that number is 18 inches. You will be placing the four PVC pipes into the ground in a rectangle that measures 18 x 36 x 18 x 36 inches. Mark those locations on the ground.

4. Dig four holes, about six inches deep.

5. Place a PVC pipe in each hole.

6. Stand your ladders up into these PVC supports.

7. Add sand, gravel, or cement to hold the ladders in place.

8. Drop the short ladder over the top of the two uprights. Secure it with a screw or two.

9. How does it look? Good? Congratulations. Imagine what it will look like covered by your favorite vines!

10. Here are a few variations:

a. Make the top ladder 36 inches long, and mortise and tenon it into the two upright ladders. Drill holes into the face of each ladder post at 98 inches, measured up from the bottom.

b. Does it wiggle? Add a few curved braces.

c. Does it look too bare? Add a few decorative pieces all over the arbor.

d. Add a bench by making two more ladders, each 36 inches high, with rungs at 16 inches and 24 inches.

e. Make an arbor using nailed (face-jointed) ladders. Every step is the same.

PANEL CHAIRS

A good way to sneak up on the challenges of chairmaking is to make a panel chair. A chair made from two panels can serve as a model for deciding what you like and want to change about the next chair.

First, construct a ladder that is 45 inches tall. Position the first rung 7 inches up from the floor, the next at 15 inches, the next at 20 inches, and the last at 40 inches. Use rungs that are 16 inches long. This modified ladder will give you the rung positioning for the seat and back supports of a chair. You may want to vary these numbers somewhat when you build other chairs of this type.

For the front, make a small panel measuring 24 inches tall, with the first rung positioned at 7 inches and the second at 15 inches. Again, use rungs that are 16 inches long. Many chairs are trapezoids, with the front measuring up to four inches wider than the back. This front rung could be 20 inches long, if necessary.

Join the two panels with 16-inch long rungs, attached 9 inches and 16 inches from the floor.

The front legs have been left long enough to accept arms. If you don't want arms, saw them off after the chair has been glued together and has dried. To complete the chair, take a look at the discussions of finishing and seating on pages 43 to 46.

PANEL BENCHES

This panel bench is a very simple design in which the top rung is also the back support. This bench doesn't have any twiggy designs in it and can be made from any kinds of wood. The seat is rough cut wood, screwed into the front and back panels to create a rigid form.

This particular panel bench is 36 inches high and 48 inches wide. The top rail in the back is positioned 27 inches from the floor and the next ones down are at 14 inches and 7 inches. The front panel has just one rung, positioned 15 inches from the floor. The side rungs are at 9 inches and 21 inches. I do not glue these pieces together. I clamp them and put a screw through the joints.

A panel bench is a very good way to learn to make a rustic bed. Just imagine the side rungs stretched out about 6 feet: there, a bed! For a twin-size bed, use rungs 38 inches wide; for a full size, use rungs 54 inches wide; for queen size, use rungs 60 inches; for king size, use rungs 76 inches wide (and beefy). For side rails, the twin and full use 80-inch-long rungs, and the queen- and king-size beds use 84-inch-long rungs.

gallery *of* PANEL-BASED WORK

LEFT: Screen, Daniel Mack

BELOW: Bookcase and details,
Daniel Mack

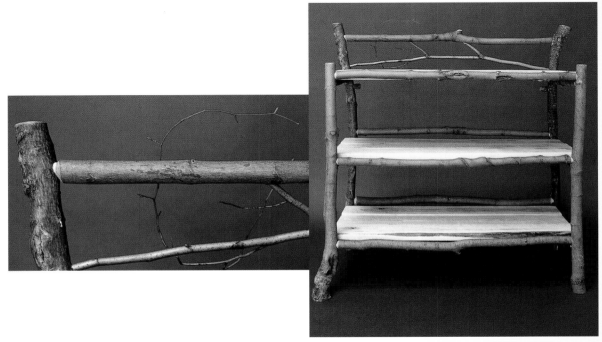

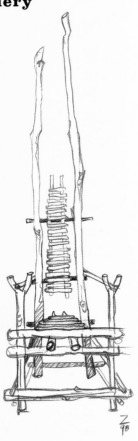

LEFT: Bookcase, Daniel Mack

BELOW: Birch-bark bookcase, Steven Walsh

BOTTOM LEFT: Bookcase, Daniel Mack

LEFT: Pine and oleander twig screen, Gordon Grabe

BELOW: Screen, Tor Faegre

Tables

THE SECRET CHARM OF TABLES

I have been building tables almost as long as I have been making chairs. What I have found is that their function seems to overwhelm the possibility of charm. They can be sturdy, useful, handsome, well-designed, well-made, and even beautiful, but it is difficult to create a table that has the same magic as a chair.

For a while, I was quite prejudiced against tables. They were so simple, so plain. They didn't have the buzz of a Chair. However, over time I have learned that their simplicity hides a wonderful lesson. For something to have magic or charm—or meaning—there has to be a process of "charging." The item has to be around and be used, and by that very fact it comes to reflect and hold personal meaning. This is why someone keeps an ill-proportioned, scuffed-up, wiggley side table made in a factory in the 1920s. It's because it was the table that always sat next to grandfather's chair. Period.

So by your afternoon of Making you have begun the "charging" process for your family. You may be the object of teasing, admiration, envy. You may feel the flush of embarrassment when the neighbor-cabinetmaker visits. Or a giddy rush of delight when he says "I wish I could make something like that." These are all indications that life is going on.

The tables I am describing here are merely ways of seducing you into becoming a Maker. After your first success, you will have this object, this little defenseless table that you made. It will need a home, a place. It will begin to generate stories around itself—stories of you, of making—and stories are what hold life together. It may not be The Greatest Story Ever Told...but how many of them can there be?

In this section of the book you will find three different approaches to making tables. You will no doubt discover many more of your own.

Plank-style table,
Daniel Mack

How big are tables?
As big as you want!

Tables are somewhat more standard than chairs, although they should cooperate with the needs of the user and the surrounding furniture. Key decisions for dining tables involve the distance to set back the legs from the ends and sides to give stability yet allow for easy sitting on the ends and sides. Each person should have 24 inches of tabletop and the apron should be 24 inches from the floor. Another variable is the finished height from the floor; this varies from 29 to 31 inches. Often rustic tables include roots and twisted branches that eat up available space and diminish the utility of the table.

DINING TABLES
Sample size and seating capacity

rectangular tables

L" X W"	SEATING
120 x 48	1–12 people
108 x 48	8–10 people
84 x 42	8 people
72 x 36	6 people
60 x 30	4 people

round tables

DIAMETER	SEATING
60" round	7–8 people
48" round	5–6 people
42" round	4–5 people

square tables

L" X W"	SEATING
60 x 60	8–12 people
54 x 54	6–8 people
48 x 48	6–8 people
42 x 42	4 people
36 x 36	4 people

OTHER TABLES

	HEIGHT	LENGTH	WIDTH
Coffee	14–18"	min. 24"	min. 20"
Sofa Table	26–31"	min. 60"	12–18"
Side Table	19–21"	24"	8"
Nightstand	21–27"	min. 12"	min. 12"
Desk	29–30"	min. 54"	min. 24"

BASIC PLANT STAND

This is a simple plant stand or side table measuring 12 inches square on top and 21 inches tall. To make it, you can use any type of flat top. You might have an old breadboard, cabinet door, piece of marble or Formica. Everybody has flat things hidden somewhere. Tables from early in this century were made from parts of orange crates. These would make an excellent tabletop. Be resourceful. Potential tabletops are everywhere.

What You Do

1. Drill holes in the top. Depending on your sense of design and the size of your table, either a ⅝-inch hole or a 1-inch hole will work. The holes can go straight into the wood or at an angle. I sometimes use a drill press, but a hand-held drill is just fine, too.

2. Cut tenons on one end of each of the four legs. The tenons can be made in any of the ways described in this book (see pages 40 to 42).

3. Glue and/or nail the legs into the top.

4. After you've put the legs in, the table may still wiggle. You can use diagonals or angled cross pieces to steady up the table.

5. Now, even though the table is stable, it may not stand quite straight because one of the legs may be a little long. Is there never any end to these rustic surprises? Hang the long leg over the edge of the worktable, and mark with a pencil how much of it hangs off. Cut off that little wedge or coin size piece with a handsaw, or if it's really small, use a rasp to take it off.

What You Need

TABLETOP MEASURING
12 x 12 INCHES*

4 saplings, at least 2 inches in diameter, and about 20 inches long

tape measure

drill with ⅝- or 1-inch bit

tenon-cutting tools

rubber mallet

wood glue

hammer

finishing nails

pencil

handsaw or rasp

* This tabletop is a 2 x 12-inch piece of pine from a lumberyard.

SIMPLE
PANEL TABLE

*S*ometimes *I approach a table as if it's a chair with a flat top. This means I can use the panel method of building discussed on page 59. I have made this table by connecting two panels or ladders, similar to the bookcase on page 61. What you have to watch for is the leg and kick room needed for a table, which means that sometimes the stretchers are in the center of the piece. Susan Nagel built this table in a day.*

What You Need

4 legs cut from 4-inch saplings, each about 18 inches long

8 pieces for the stretchers, each about 4 inches wide and 24 inches long

1 x 12 finished planed oak boards, ½ inch thick

4–6 battens, pieces of 1 x 3-inch wood

tape measure

cutting tools

tenon-cutting tools

rubber mallet

circular saw or jigsaw

drill with assorted bits

carpenter's glue

pipe clamps, bar clamps or web-strap clamps

sander grinder, rasp, or sandpaper

hammer

nails

screwdriver

screws

sandpaper

linseed oil

mineral spirits

wood stain or polyurethane

paintbrush

What You Do

1. The frame is made using the panel method described on page 59. Once you have test-fitted the panel, glue up the frame. Carpenter's glue needs to set under pressure, so it's good to clamp your frames together. Some people make a tourniquet-like clamp from rope or rubber tubing.

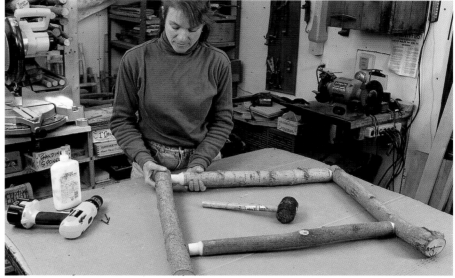

2. With a circular saw or jigsaw, trim the oak boards so they fit the size and shape of your base. You may want to round the edges with a sander-grinder, rasp, or just sandpaper to help the wood look more rustic.

3. Attach the two oak boards to one another using battens screwed on from the bottom side. Using battens for this purpose replicates the design used in old barn doors, where several small pieces of wood running perpendicular to others hold everything together. The battens can be screwed in or nailed on. Usually the boards are held tightly together with clamps while the battens are being put on.

4. Screw on the top through oversized holes on the stretchers.

5. Lightly sand the frame and the legs. Then apply the mixture of 50/50 linseed oil and mineral spirits.

6. If you like, add your own embellishments such as moldings, slices of pinecone, small mosaics of twig, bark appliqué, etc.

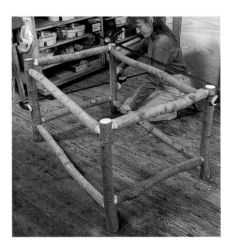

APRON TABLE

A*nother way to make a table is to create a rigid box or apron for the table. To this structure you first add the legs and then you attach the top. I have built this type of table many times. It's sturdy and invites quite a bit of custom decoration.*

What You Need

materials for the apron *

tabletop

4 legs of dried forked branches, about 2–3 inches at the butt and about 40 inches long

2 stretchers of the same or similar 2 x 4 lumber as the material used for the apron. (These will never be seen, but must take a lot of screws and nails.)

1 center stretcher of 2-inch sapling, about 36 inches long

8 diagonal supports cut from curvy 1-inch saplings, each 18 inches long

tape measure

cutting tools

tenon-cutting tools

rubber mallet

drill and assorted bits

screws

screwdriver

rasp

hammer

nails

handsaw or sander-grinder

boiled linseed oil

mineral spirits

butcher's wax (from local supermarket)

tung oil (optional)

0000 steel wool (optional)

* This can be any kind of 2 x 4 lumber. I've also used old studding from houses and cedar 2 x 4s from fencing suppliers. You need material with enough beef that it can handle a lot of things being screwed or nailed into it and still keep its shape and strength. The size of the apron will depend on the size of the tabletop. It should be about 6 inches smaller than the tabletop.

What You Do

1. Cut the wood for the apron, making sure the assembled apron will be about 6 inches smaller than the top. This allows for a little bit of overhang, 3 inches all around, so you can still see the apron, which may have some interesting decoration on it.

2. To assemble the apron, you can butt joint the pieces. The apron shown here has mitered corners. The pieces were then glued and screwed together with trim screws.

(Screws? Why screws? Isn't this supposed to be big-time fancy rustic art? The great thing about using screws with rustic work is that, if you don't like what you've built, you can undo it and try something else.)

3. Add two stretchers, each about 5 inches from the center of the apron. These are the two main supports for the branch legs. Use screws to attach them to the apron.

4. Pair up the four legs to make sure you know how you want them to be positioned. Trim the top edge of each fork so it will fit flat against the stretcher.

5. Screw one pair of legs into one of the stretchers. Repeat this process with the second pair of legs and the other stretcher.

6. Once all the legs are positioned, cross-screw them through the apron. Use screws to secure. Trim-head screws work well.

7. Add a center stretcher or crosspiece to connect the two pairs of legs. When you're done assembling the table, you may want to trim off a few inches of the overhang.

8. Start to level the legs by first measuring up from a level, flat surface; then trim them as flat as you can by eye.

Note: A week after I made this table, I decided I didn't like the way the diagonals looked in relation to each other. So I spent a few hours rearranging them.

9. Add eight diagonal supports between the legs and the apron. This steadies up the entire form and makes it rigid enough to do the final leveling with either a saw or a sander-grinder, if you've gotten within a ¼-inch of level.

10. Put the top on and attach with tabletop hardware.

11. To finish the table, sand and oil the base with two coats of boiled linseed oil, cut 50/50 with mineral spirits. Then wax it.

12. I went a little further to finish the table; this step is optional. Apply four coats of tung oil on the top over a four-day period, lightly sanding between coats with 0000 steel wool. Then wax the top again.

GNARLED BASES

Another way to make a table is to find or create a beautiful base. I have done this many times over and I've ended up with very unusual tables—or sometimes no table—just a great base.

Here is a base made from the roots of a maple tree that fell over in a creek in the Catskills. I collected this one in 1979.

Watch what happens when three different tops are used with the same base: the entire feel of the table changes. To this day, I cannot decide what to put on this base.

gallery *of* TABLES

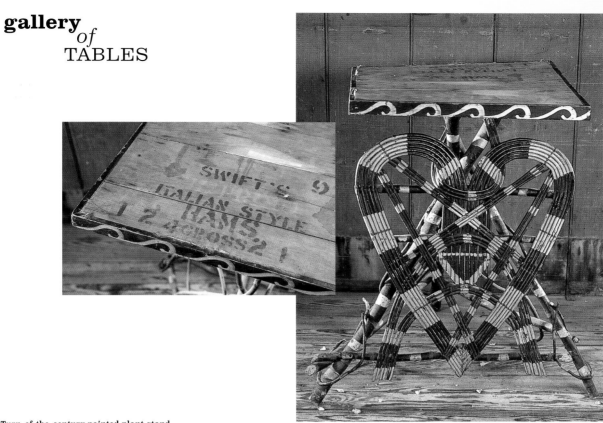

ABOVE: Turn-of-the-century painted plant stand with found wood tabletop

BELOW: Table, Greg Mitchell

BELOW RIGHT: Table, Daniel Mack, Robert Kalka

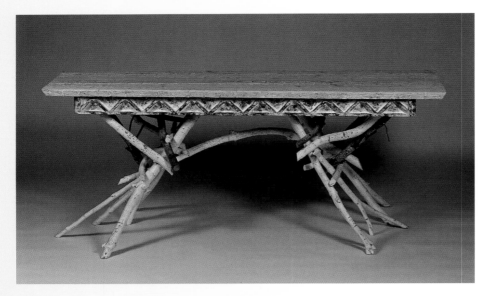

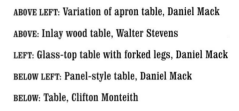

ABOVE LEFT: Variation of apron table, Daniel Mack

ABOVE: Inlay wood table, Walter Stevens

LEFT: Glass-top table with forked legs, Daniel Mack

BELOW LEFT: Panel-style table, Daniel Mack

BELOW: Table, Clifton Monteith

ABOVE: Slate top table, Daniel Mack

ABOVE RIGHT: Birch table, Tom Phillips

RIGHT: Beaver-chewed driftwood table, Daniel Mack

BELOW RIGHT: Apron-style coffee table, Daniel Mack

BELOW: Plant stand with forks, Daniel Mack

Rustic Festival

OTHER RUSTIC STYLES

By now, my style of building in linear-rectilinear forms should be quite clear...even too clear. Although that is the style I am drawn to for my work, I have a great deal of appreciation for other rustic styles. There are many ways to make rustic furniture and many that haven't yet been discovered.

To illustrate this point, I invited eight talented rustics—some are weekend builders and some have rustic businesses—to come to my shop for a couple of days so we could all make things and watch how we each worked. It was a very pleasant time. And indeed, it did give us all the opportunity to observe different ways of rustic thinking and making in action. Here's a look at that weekend.

EIGHT RUSTIC MAKERS
AND THEIR WORK

Barbara cut all her pieces to size, and then carefully drills and tenons them with the new tenon-cutting accessory from Lee Valley Tools.

BARBARA HARMEYER is presently the general contractor on her new house. She has taught art, photography, and video, and likes rustic work because it's "so direct." She built several tables using local white birch. Barbara is intrigued by the subtlety of color in the various birches. Some of the tables she builds are free-form. Others, like the one shown here, are quite planned out.

She uses thin twigs for the tabletops, gluing them into the drilled holes, and clamping the pieces until the assembly is dry.

STEVE WALSH is the superintendent of a grounds crew. He has always been an outdoors person and volunteers with the Boy Scouts. He builds rustic work only when he has a particular gift to make for someone. He prefers white birch, out of which he has built bookcases and these special frames. The process is very much like veneering, where pieces of bark are very carefully cut and glued onto wood with rubber cement.

For intricate designs, Steve numbers each section of the plywood, then numbers the backs of the corresponding pieces of bark. He carefully glues the bark to the plywood frame with rubber cement.

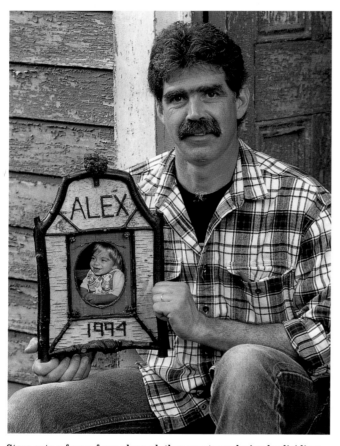

Steve cuts a frame from plywood, then creates a design by dividing the frame into symmetrical sections. He measures the bark to fit and cuts it out.

Using pruning shears and a sharp craft knife, Steve outlines the bark sections of the design. He lightly draws letters onto the bark, then cuts and tacks short segments of split twigs to create writing.

Steve uses contact cement and, for the larger pieces, finish nails, to attach the sticks to the bark-covered frame. To finish the frame, he sprays on several coats of clear polyurethane.

MICHELLE ELLSWORTH has a background that includes drawing, sign painting, and work with fabric. She shows her works at Renaissance Faires. She builds in a stick style using local New Jersey woods. Her footstool is a combination of upholstered comfort and simplicity. Her preferred work style uses the floor and ground as support.

After padding the seat and covering it with upholstery fabric, she glues the legs into the holes in the upholstered frame.

Michelle holds each leg in a vise while she cuts the tenon with a tenon cutter. Then she uses a saw to level the bottoms of each leg. She cuts the seat from plywood and drills holes through the board to match the size of the tenons.

JUDITH POEHLER lives in a city apartment, and has chosen to make rustic work of appropriate scale. She collects branches that have small, interesting knots and forks. She buys old utensils in antique shops or new ones in houseware stores. Then she carves the pieces of wood until she has created useful and beautiful handles for flatware. There is a gentle rhythm to this work which you can feel in the finished pieces.

Judith uses a sharp knife to carve the hardwood pieces until a pleasing shape appears. Then she cuts a groove for the utensil and wedges it tightly into the handle. To finish the pieces, she sands the wood and applies several coats of linseed oil.

CHUCK FREDERICKS, a woodworker and wood carver, started his rustic business, WoodChuck Enterprises, in 1989, in Forestburgh, New York. Using local materials, Chuck offers rustic furniture, ranging from miniature high chairs for teddy bears to large porch swings. Characteristic of his work is the combination of lumber-milled wood and tree branches. He enjoys combining a number of different types of wood in the same piece.

This bench has a top made from lumber-milled white pine, legs made from peeled Canadian white cedar, and decorative diagonals that combine a variety of woods, including maple, pine, black birch, and white pine.

The legs are joined to the top with mortise and tenon joints. Chuck aligns and adjusts the legs until the bench is stable, then he attaches the ends and the crosspieces. To the finished top, Chuck applies a golden oak stain. Then he coats the entire piece with acrylic polyurethane.

LAURA SPECTOR started building rustic furniture in 1993, using vines she cuts from the wisteria trees that grow in abundance in her area of Connecticut. Laura's benches remind her of the furniture she saw on family childhood vacations at Lake Mohonk, near New Paltz, New York. She brings a dancer's sensibility to her building. Her work reflects the "arcs, flow, twirls, and flexibility of dance." Laura is building a rustic business, selling these dramatic vine pieces.

Laura uses a bow saw to cut the vines into useable segments of varying lengths.

She attaches scrap lumber boards to the vine frame to create a seat for the bench. Although she uses a compressed air-driven nailer to attach the boards and the twisted vines, she has found this tool to be very dangerous, and advises caution when using it.

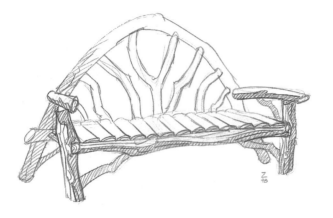

Laura doesn't know what the finished piece will actually look like until she sees it emerge from the twisted vines. So she builds and unbuilds, tries and re-tries, until she is pleased with the results.

By weaving, twisting, and sometimes wrestling the vines into the structure, she creates tension which makes the whole piece sturdy.

Laura trims off any stray vines with toppers.

MARK NIMAL, who works in a state park, grew up in rural Maine, and has always loved the woods, gardening, and "foraging." At his job he operates heavy machinery. Perhaps this is why he looks for ways to adapt various power tools and regular carpentry methods for rustic work. The settee and chairs shown here are based on a style of rustic Mission furniture, originally designed by Old Hickory Furniture.

Mark joins the pieces together using dowels. Into each side of a joint he drills a hole the size of the dowel, then glues the dowel into the holes with carpenter's glue. This makes a very strong union.

From salvaged chestnut beams, Mark cut the pieces with a band saw.

Mark taught himself to weave split oak seats from materials he buys from seating-supply houses.

Here he staples two oak splits together before continuing to weave.

ANDREW GARDNER has a background in graphic design and knows just how he wants his bentwood furniture to turn out—strong and elegant. Nails, a hammer, and a saw are his basic tools for creating this attractive furniture. Andy sells his work at craft shows and at a few local stores and galleries. He has been kind enough to provide very thorough directions (see the following page) for building a chair in his style.

BENTWOOD ARMCHAIR

DESIGNER/BUILDER: ANDREW GARDNER

What You Need

FOR THE CHAIR FRAME

2 front legs: 2 x 16 inches

2 back legs: 2 x 32 inches

8 pieces 1½ x 24 to 26 inches

3 Y-shaped pieces: 1½ x 24 to 26 inches, 15 inches from base to fork

2 pieces 1½ x 26 to 28 inches

1 piece ¾ x 26 inches

2 pieces 1¼ x 48 inches

14 reasonably straight pieces, 4 to 5 feet long, 1 inch at base

7 reasonably straight pieces, 6 to 7 feet long, 1 inch at base

20 straight pieces, 4 to 5 feet long, ½ inch at base

18- or 21-inch bow saw

anvil-style hand pruner/cutters

small Stanley Surform rasp

16-ounce carpenter's hammer

nail set (or drift punch)

spring clamps (optional)

hacksaw

flat bastard file

drill and assorted bits

tape measure

nails: 8d, 10d, 12d twisted, galvanized decking or patio nails; 1 and 1⅝-inch annular ribbed shank panel or hardboard nails

What You Do

Building the Basic Frame

1. The first step is to collect the willow, or "swamp willow," which can be found along most rivers and streams. This bush type plant is incredibly strong for its weight, quite flexible even when seasoned, and doesn't split when nailed. Also, once the willow has aged, insects will not move in. Each piece must be reasonably straight. Willow is a renewable resource that thrives with cutting.

2. Join the front and back legs with two horizontal pieces, 1½ x 24 to 26 inches (figure 1). The one on top should be Y-shaped, with the Y towards the back. The front end should be about 1½ inches below the top of the front leg. The bottom piece should be about 5 inches from the floor. Use two nails at each point of contact, excluding the lower branch of the Y.

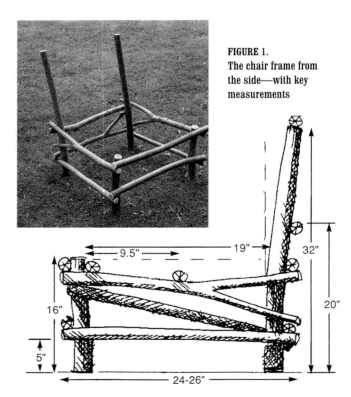

FIGURE 1.
The chair frame from the side—with key measurements

3. Make sure the seat drops slightly from front to rear—1 to 2 inches at the most. Notice, also how the back slopes away from the front—again no more than about 2 inches.

4. Make a mirror copy of this first side.

5. Join the two sides together in front with two horizontal pieces of the same size. The top support should rest on top of the Y pieces. Secure the back in the same manner as the sides, with a Y piece on top and a straight 24- to 26-inch piece on the bottom.

6. To make the frame rigid, nail a diagonal brace from front to rear on both sides of the chair (figure 2). Start by nailing these to the outside top of the front legs. Then straighten the chair to give it the symmetric shape you desire. Now you can nail each diagonal brace to the bottom inside of the back legs. Again, use two nails at each point of contact.

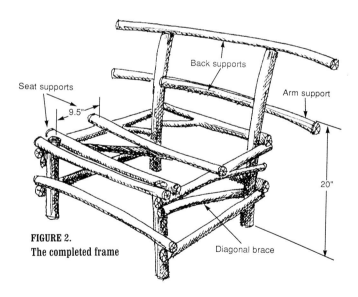

Seat supports
9.5"
Back supports
Arm support
20"
Diagonal brace

FIGURE 2.
The completed frame

7. Nail the second branch of the Y pieces to the back legs (figure 2).

8. Place another 1½ x 24- to 26-inch piece directly behind the front legs, on top of the Y pieces. Secure with two nails at each contact point as before.

9. Nail another piece of the same size in the same manner, halfway between the front and back legs.

10. Cut a piece to fit securely between the back legs. Nail it in between the legs, 20 inches off the floor. This is called the back spreader.

11. Immediately behind the back spreader, secure one of the 48-inch pieces for an arm support.

12. Secure the other 48-inch piece on top of the back legs.

13. Set all the nails, and cut off the exposed nail ends.

14. Trim off any excess wood and bevel all cut ends with the Surform.

15. Now sit on the frame. Is it sturdy? Your seat should fall slightly behind the middle bar and your shoulders probably will touch the top of the back support.

Creating the Arms

The arms are built cane by cane so that any stress placed on the frame is uniformly spread across the chair. Because these branches are a bit more delicate than those in the frame, you may want to predrill nail holes as you go (in case you're not sure where each randomly placed cane will wind up).

1. Flex each cane to limber it up a bit before starting.

2. Maneuver the first cane from the inside lower front up to the top of the arm support (figure 3).

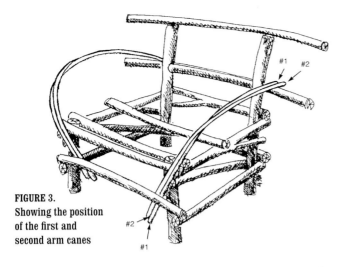

FIGURE 3.
Showing the position
of the first and
second arm canes

#1 #2

#2

#1

3. Nail this first piece, using long panel nails, in three places: on top of the arm support, in front of the seat stop, and behind the lower horizontal support. Leave the nail heads exposed so you can remove them later, if necessary.

4. Position the second cane next to the first at the bottom front support; place the other end next to the first on the arm support. Make sure the canes are touching along their entire length (see figure 3).

5. Beginning with the second cane, nail each to the frame and to its neighbor, using both long and short panel nails.

6. When the last arm cane is in place, drive in and set the nails.

Wrapping the Back of the Chair

When placing subsequent canes, alternate which side you started the base of the cane.

1. Hook the first cane under the arm and over the top of the frame. Bend the cane so that the other end can be placed under the opposite arm (see figure 4).

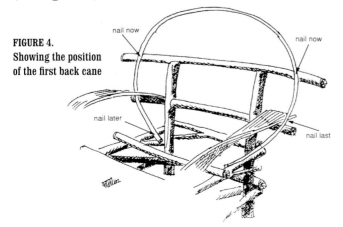

nail now

nail now

FIGURE 4.
Showing the position
of the first back cane

nail later

nail last

2. Nail the cane only to the top horizontal piece on the back of each side.

3. Add the other canes in the same manner, nailing each new cane to the top of the previous ones at 6- to 8-inch intervals.

4. Once all the back canes are in place, the ends can be trimmed uniformly and spread out at equal intervals from the back leg to the center seat support. Nail each one into place. Also nail the canes where they come into firm contact with the arms.

5. Sit down in the chair and see how rigid it has become.

Constructing the Seat

1. Measure and mark the center point on the seat support between the front legs. Repeat this process with the center seat support and the back support.

2. Cut a piece ¾ inch in diameter, slightly shorter than the top front frame piece.

3. Place this piece on top of the front seat support against the top of the leg. Nail it into position about every 3 inches with nails at opposing angles (see figure 5). This "seat stop" conceals the front ends of the seat canes and helps to keep them from rising up when you sit in the chair.

4. Next, select a uniform seat cane and flex it a bit. Place the leaf end up behind the back and lay it along one side of the center line (see figure 5). Nail it first in front and then in the middle.

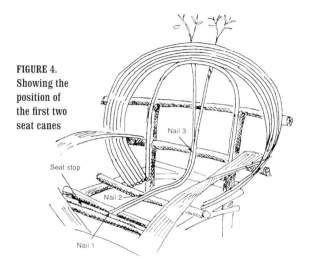

FIGURE 4. Showing the position of the first two seat canes

Nail 3

Seat stop

Nail 2

Nail 1

5. Press the cane down slightly just before it curves up the back, and nail it to the lower back support.

6. Place the second cane next to the first and repeat the nailing process.

7. Place the third cane slightly more than 1 inch from the first and nail it as you did the first two.

8. Place the fourth cane next to the second, etc. The seat canes can be paired at intervals throughout or interspersed with single canes.

9. Once you have finished securing the seat canes, spread them out in a fashion that suits you, and nail them to the upper back support.

10. Drive in any unsecured nails, set them, and trim up the back.

11. On the back side, nail the top of the seat canes three times each to different back canes at opposing angles.

12. Sit down, rest, and enjoy your handiwork!

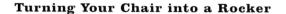

Turning Your Chair into a Rocker

A rocker is built the same way as the chair except that the legs are two inches shorter. Pattern the runner, or rocker, after one you know rocks well for you. Yellow pine stair tread is a good wood to use, and is available at most larger lumberyards.

1. Trace the pattern on the wood, and free-cut with a saber saw.

2. Dress the edges and stain the wood with three coats of oil stain.

3. Place the runner on the outside of the legs, with only the pointed end extending beyond the front leg. Draw a line on the leg where the runner meets.

4. Turn the chair upside down and place a straight board on its edge, from front to back leg down the middle. This ensures the alignment of the runner.

5. Draw a line on each leg bottom along this line, dividing the leg in half. Extend these lines along the legs, beyond the side mark for the runner.

6. Carefully sawing, cut from the side runner marks to the halfway marks. Then either chisel or saw down to the saw cut.

7. Lay the rocker in place and check for fit, adjusting as needed with a chisel.

8. When the rocker and legs fit reasonably well, clamp them in place and drill a ¼-inch hole through the middle of each leg and rocker where they join.

9. Connect your rockers to your chair with ¼ x 2½-inch round head or carriage bolts with hex nuts and washers on both sides.

10. Sit down and rock your cares away!

gallery *of* CONTEMPORARY RUSTIC WORK

ABOVE: Rocking Chair, Gabriel Casey

LEFT: Grandfather clock, Jay Dawson

BELOW: Willow Cove Chairs, willow and red birch, Don C. King

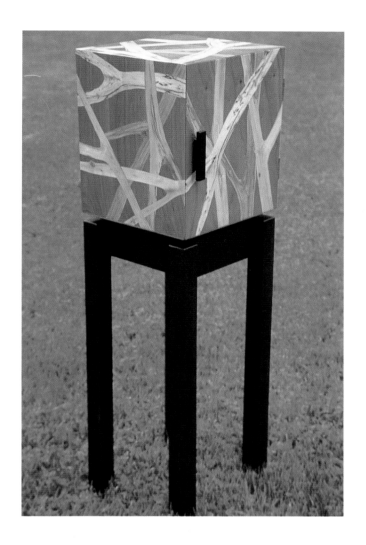

ABOVE LEFT: The Magician's Box, maple, ash, and Chinese chestnut twigs on cherry background, Walter Stevens

ABOVE: Wall sconce, cherry with birch shade, Jerry Womacks

LEFT: Desk and chair, James Hanley

ABOVE: Table lamp, osage orange base, Jerry Womacks

ABOVE RIGHT: Desk, James Hanley

RIGHT: Driftwood chairs and settee, Bruce Cagwin

ABOVE: Wall clock, cherry
with twig inlay and painting,
Jerry Womacks

ABOVE LEFT: Chair #3,
Susan Parish

LEFT: Bench, Susan Parish

ABOVE: Chair with woven back and seat, Dirk Leach

ABOVE RIGHT: Chair with roots, Jonah Meyer

RIGHT: Chair, Dirk Leach

BELOW: Bark and twig clock, Jerry and Jessica Farrell

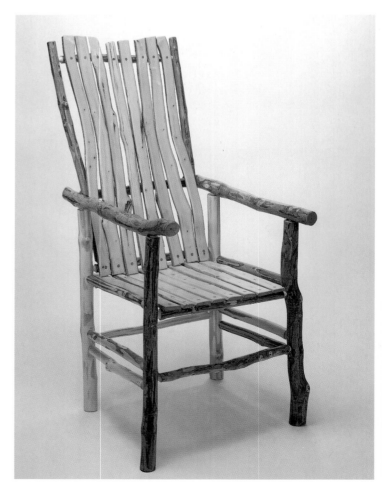

ABOVE LEFT: Twig mosaic table, Todd Barrow

LEFT: Transplantation, plum branches, Jack Sewell

BELOW: Tree of Life, Jim Cameron

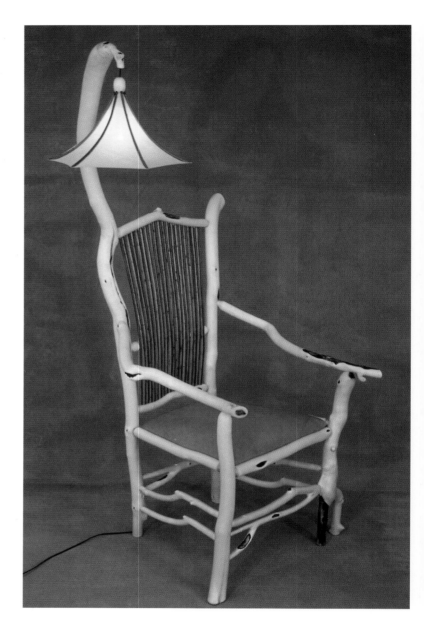

ABOVE LEFT: Chair, Charles Fahr

ABOVE: Chaise Avec Fleur, maple and willow, Don C. King

LEFT: Lamp, Clifton Monteith

ABOVE LEFT: Nurseryman's Desk, English walnut, recycled pine boards, Gordon Grabe.
PHOTO BY RITA NICHOLAS

ABOVE: Juniper chair, Brent McGregor

LEFT: Twig mosaic settee, Todd Barrow

ABOVE: Twig mosaic table, Sharon Ladd

LEFT: Bentwood lounge, Nick Parker

ABOVE: Twig mosaic bureau, Todd Barrow

ABOVE RIGHT: Bentwood chair, Richard Lee

BELOW AND BELOW RIGHT: Chairs by Maxwell Newhouse

RUSTIC RESOURCES

CLASSES IN RUSTIC AND TRADITIONAL WOODWORKING /CRAFTS

BENTWOOD BUILDING
summer classes
with Michael Emmons
Center for Furniture
Craftmanship
125 West Meadow Road
Rockport, ME 04841
tel: **207-236-4737**

TRADITIONAL COUNTRY WOODWORKING
classes year-round
with Drew Langsner
Country Workshops
90 Mill Creek Road
Marshall, NC 28753
e-mail:
langsner@madison.main.nc.us

RUSTIC BUILDING FOR BEGINNERS AND ADVANCED MAKERS
1-2-5-day workshops
with Daniel Mack
Daniel Mack Rustic Furnishing
14 Welling Avenue
Warwick, NY 10990
tel: **914-986-7293**
e-mail: **rustic@warwick.net**
website: www.**danielmack.com**

RUSTIC EVENTS

CELEBRATE NATURE: A RUSTIC FESTIVAL
(in Spring)
Museum Village
Rt 17M
Monroe, NY 10950
tel: **914-986-7293**

RUSTIC MAKERS DAY
(in September)
Adirondack Museum
Blue Mountain Lake, NY 12812
tel: **518-352-7311**
fax: **518-352-7653**

MUSEUMS WITH RUSTIC FURNITURE

ADIRONDACK MUSEUM
PO Box 99
Blue Mountain Lake, NY 12812
tel: **518-352-7311**

BUFFALO BILL MUSEUM
720 Sheridan Avenue
Cody, WY 82414
tel: **307-587-4771**

HENRY FORD MUSEUM
20900 Oakwood Blvd.
Dearborn, MI 48121
tel: **313-271-1620**

SHELBURNE MUSEUM
PO Box 10, Route 7
Shelburne, VT 05482
tel: **802-985-3344**

WESTERN HERITAGE CENTER
2822 Montana Avenue
Billings, MT 59101
tel: **406-256-6809**

RUSTIC STYLE LODGES

BIG CEDAR LODGE
612 Devil's Pool Road
Ridgedale, MO 65739
tel: **417-335-2777**

LAKE PLACID LODGE
White Face Inn Road
PO Box 550
Lake Placid, NY 12946
tel: **518-523-2700**

MOHONK MOUNTAIN HOUSE
Lake Mohonk
New Paltz, NY 12561
tel: **914-255-1000**

THE POINT
HCR1 Box 65
Saranac Lake, NY 12983
tel: **518-891-5674**

POST RANCH INN
PO Box 219
Big Sur, CA 93920
tel: **408-667-2200**

THE SWAG
Rt 2, Box 280-A
Waynesville, NC 28786
tel: **828-926-0430**

ORGANIZATIONS

EARLY AMERICAN INDUSTRIES ASSOCIATION
PO Box 143
Delmar, NY 12054
fax: **518-439-1066**
website:
ourworld.compuserve.com/ homepages/oldtools/about.htm

THE FURNITURE SOCIETY
PO Box 18
Free Union, VA 22940
tel: **804-973-1488**
website:
monticello.avenue.gen.va.us/ arts/furniture/

AMERICAN SOCIETY OF FURNITURE ARTISTS
PO Box 35339
Houston, TX 77235
tel: **713-721-7600**
website: **www.asof.org**

RUSTIC MATERIALS

GOOD WOOD LTD.
Rt 2, Box 447A
Bethel, VT 05032
tel: **802-234-5534**
e-mail: **goodwood@sover.net**
Offers birch and birch bark

JERRY FARRELL
PO Box 255
Sidney Center, NY 13839
tel: **607-369-4916**
Offers birch bark and woods of the Northeast

INTERMARES TRADING CO.
Box 617
Lindenhurst, NY 11757
tel: **800-229-2263**
Offers bamboo, cane, and materials from Asia

SEATING SUPPLIES/MATERIALS

THE CANING SHOP
926 Gilman Street
Berkeley, CA 94710
tel: **514-527-5010**

CONNECTICUT CANE AND REED
PO Box 762B
Manchester, CT 06040
tel: **203-646-6586**

HANCOCK SHAKER VILLAGE
PO Box 898
Pittsfield, MA 01202
tel: **413-443-0188**

H.H. PERKINS COMPANY
10 South Bradley Road
Woodbridge, CT 06525
tel: **203-389-9501**

PLYMOUTH REED & CANE
1200 W. Ann Arbor Road
Plymouth, MI 48170
tel: **313-455-2150**

SHAKER WORKSHOPS
PO Box 1028
Concord, MA 01742
tel: **617-646-8985**

SHAKERTOWN AT PLEASANT HILL, INC.
3500 Lexington Road
Harrodsburg, KY 40330
tel: **606-734-5411**

STURGES MANUFACTURING
Box 55
Utica, NY 13503
tel: **315-732-6159**
($750 minimum order)

THE UNFINISHED UNIVERSE
525 W. Short Street
Lexington, KY 40507
tel: **606-252-3289**

NEW TOOLS AND TOOL CATALOGS

LEE VALLEY TOOLS
12 East River Street
Ogdensburg, NY 13669
tel: **800-871-8158** *or* **613-596-0350**
Free catalog
Offers affordable tenon cutters, very inventive tools, drill bits, and books

MLCS
PO Box 4053/C-25
Rydal, PA 19046
tel: **800-533-9298**
Free catalog
Offers tenon cutters and clamps

JESADA TOOLS
310 Mears Blvd.
Oldsmar, FL 34677
tel: **800-531-5559**
Free catalog
Offers cutters and bits

BRIDGE CITY TOOL WORKS
1104 NE 28th Avenue
Portland, OR 97232
tel: **503-282-6997**
Free catalog
Offers many specialized and beautiful tools

HARTVILLE TOOL AND SUPPLY
940 West Maple Street
Hartville, OH 44632
tel: **800-345-2396**
Free catalog
Offers specialized woodworking tools and air cleaners

VAN DYKE'S SUPPLIERS
PO Box 278
Woonsocket, SD 57385
tel: **605-796-4425**
Free catalog
Offers furniture hardware

WOODCRAFT SUPPLY CORP.
210 Wood County
 Industrial Park
Parkersburg, WV 26102
tel: **800-225-1153** *or* **304-428-4866**
Free catalog
Offers most woodworking tools

WOODWORKERS SUPPLY
21108 North Glenn Road
Casper, WY 82601
tel: **307-237-5354**
Free catalog
Offers finer woodworking tools

SPECIALIZED TOOLS

Low-temperature Kilns

NYLE CORPORATION
PO Box 1107
Bangor, ME 04401
tel: **800-777-6953**

EBAC LUMBER DRYERS
8432 E. 33rd Street
Indianapolis, IN 46226
tel: **800-433-9011**

Tenon Cutters

LEE VALLEY TOOLS
12 East River Street
Ogdensburg, NY 13669
tel: **800-871-8158** *or* **613-596-0350**
Offers affordable tenon cutters, drill bits, and books

BRIAN BOGGS
114 Elm Street
Berea, KY 40403
tel: **606-986-9188**

BIGNELL MACHINE COMPANY
516 7th Street NE
Grand Rapids, MI 49504
tel: **616-458-2233**

MORRIS WOOD TOOL COMPANY
PO Box 249
Morristown, TN 37815-1249
tel: **615-586-0110**

Clippers, Pruners, Knives

AMERICAN STANDARD COMPANY
157 Water Street
Southington, CT 06489
tel: **203-628-9643**
Offers Rachet Action clippers and loppers

FISKARS
780 Carolina Street
Sauk City, WI 53583
tel: **800-500-4849**
Offers good folding saw and loppers

CUTCO
PO Box 810
1116 East State Street
Olean, NY 14760
Offers great whittling knives

Fasteners

McFEELEY'S SQUARE DRIVE SCREWS
1620 Wythe Road
Lynchburg, VA 24506
tel: **800-443-7937**
Offers good selection of trim-head screws and other supplies

SAMPLING OF ANTIQUE TOOL DEALERS

FALCON-WOOD
RFD 1 Box 176
Sheffield, MA 02157
tel: **413-229-7747**

MARTIN S. DONNELLY
PO Box 281
Bath, NY 14810

THE TOOL SHOP
1-3 Eagle Street
Ipswich, Sflk IP4 1JA
UK

TWO CHISELERS
1864 Glen Moor Drive
Lakewood, CO 80215
tel: **303-232-1932**

RUSTIC WOODWORKERS IN THIS BOOK

TODD BARROW
Rustic Raven
PO Box 121
Mars Hill, NC 28754

tel: **828-689-9672**
e-mail:
raven@madison.main.nc.us

ALAN BRADSTREET
Wood Wizard
856 Lawrence Road
Pownal, ME 04069

tel: **207-688-4728**

BRUCE CAGWIN
24 Hughes Road
PO Box 104
North Truro, MA 02652

tel: **508-487-3592**
fax: **508-487-3516**

JAMES CAMERON
5 Greenville Street
Hallowell, ME 04347

tel: **207-626-8505**

GABRIEL CASEY
Caherulakerla
Lisdoonvarna, Co. Clare
Ireland

tel: **353-65-74768**

**PHILLIP CRANDON
ANDREA FRANZ**
**Queen of Leaves /
Jack of Sticks**
Box 131
Palenville, NY 12463

tel: **800-347-2574** *(pin no. 81134)*

JAY DAWSON
RD1, PO Box 257
Lake Clear, NY 12945

tel: **518-891-5075**

TIM DIBBLE
Sticks and Stones
52 Tubman Road
Brewster, MA 02631

tel: **508-896-6153**

MICHELLE ELLSWORTH
39 Pleasant Valley Drive
Vernon, NJ 07462-3427

tel: **973-209-2495**

TOR FAEGERE
1600 Ashland Avenue
Evanston, IL 60201

tel: **847-869-1969**

JERRY FARRELL
PO Box 255
Sidney Center, NY

tel: **607-369-4916**

CHUCK FAHR
RR2, Box 2589
Soldier's Grove, WI 54655

tel: **608-624-5862**

CHUCK FREDERICKS
Woodchuck Enterprises
PO Box 44
Forestburgh, NY 12777

tel: **914-791-5139**

ANDREW GARDNER
RD 2, Box 25B
Thompson, PA 18465

tel: **717-727-3362**

GORDON GRABE
7680 Sonoma Hwy 12
Santa Rosa, CA 95409

tel: **707-833-6922**

website: www.angelfire.com/
ca/rusticfurniture

BARRY GREGSON
Charley Hill Road
Schroon Lake, NY 12870

tel: **518-532-9384**

JAMES HANLEY
Dancing Branch Design
PO Box 219
Eganville, ON K0J 1T0
Canada

tel: **613-628-3284**

BARBARA HARMEYER
30 Spring Lane
Chappaqua, NY 10514

tel: **914-238-0664**

TOM HOLMES
Genus International
HC01, Box 230-2
Greeley, PA 18425

tel: **717-226-6221**
fax: **717-226-1610**

SHARON KIMMELMAN
PO Box 346
New York, NY 10023

DON KING
HC 67 Box 2079
Challis, ID 83226

tel: **208-838-2449**

SHARON LADD
Willow Furnishings
216 Borden Drive
Yellow Knife, NT X1A 3R2
Canada

tel: **867-873-8646**

DIRK LEACH
18 Salmon Falls Road
PO Box 776
Bar Mills, ME 04004

tel: **207-929-5767**

RICHARD LEE
8 Winford Halstock
West Dorset, BA22 9QY
UK

tel: **01935-891-200**

DANIEL MACK
14 Welling Avenue
Warwick, NY 10990

tel: **914-986-7293**

website: www.danielmack.com/

WILLIAM McCARDLE
McCardle Rustic Furniture
7628 C.R. 381
Tyler, TX 75708

tel: **903-593-5932**

BRENT McGREGOR
**Rocky Mountain
Timber Products**
PO Box 1477
Sisters, OR 97759

tel: **541-549-1322**

JONAH MEYER
PO Box 1040
Woodstock, NY 12498

GREG MITCHELL
Legendary Furniture
1768 Woolsey Avenue
Fayetteville, AR 72703

tel: **501-521-2668**

CLIFTON MONTEITH
Box 9, 20341 East Fowler Road
Lake Ann, MI 49650

tel: **616-275-6560**

SUSAN NAGEL
60 Ormsay Street
Park Ridge, NJ 10974

MARK NIMAL
Rustics by Mark
PO Box 162
Sloatsburg, NY 10974

tel: **914-351-5260**

MAXWELL NEWHOUSE
43117 Lumsden Road
Chilliwack, BC V2R 4R5
Canada

tel: **604-683-5492**

SUSAN PARISH
2898 Glascock Street
Oakland, CA 94601

tel: **510-261-0353**

NICK PARKER
Hazel Design
Corylus Green Lane
Axminster, Devon, EX13 5TD
UK

tel: **01297-1297-35656**

TOM PHILLIPS
Star Route 2
Tupper Lake, NY 12986

tel: **518-359-9648**

JUDITH POEHLER
318 West 105 Street
New York, NY 10025

tel: **212-666-4559**

ROBBY PORTER
Deadwood Design
PO Box 65
Adamant, VT 05640

tel: **802-223-2153**

BERNADETTE SCUTARO
RD 2, Box 423
Woody Road Row
Red Hook, NY 12571

tel: **914-758-6537**

JACK SEWELL
748 W. Carson Street
Eureka, CA 95501
tel: **707-443-3896**

JEFF SNYDER
Wood-N-Wares
522 Weaver Road
Accident, MD 21520
tel: **301-746-8543**

LAURA SPECTOR
786 Westport Turnpike
Fairfield, CT 06430
tel: **203-254-3952**

WALTER STEVENS
Walter Stevens
Woodworking & Design
497 Route 55
Eldred, NY 12732
tel: **914-557-6437**

STEVEN WALSH
PO Box 252
Pawling, NY 12564
tel: **914-855-5864**

JERRY AND PAULA WOMACKS
Womacks Studio
114 Woodrow Street
Yellow Springs, OH 45387
tel: **937-767-1720**

BOOKS

Alexander, John.
*How to Build a Chair
From a Tree.*
Newtown: Taunton Press, 1981.

Brown, John.
Welsh Stick Chairs.
Fishguard, Wales: Abercastle
Publications, 1990 (and) Fresno,
CA: Linden Publishing.

Gilborn, Craig.
*Adirondack Furniture
and the Rustic Tradition.*
New York: Harry Abrams, 1987.

Kaiser, Harvey.
*Great Camps
of the Adirondacks.*
David Godine, 1982.

Kylloe, Ralph.
Rustic Traditions.
Gibbs Smith, 1993.

Langsner, Drew.
Green Woodworking.
Asheville: Lark, 1995.

Linoff, Victor. ed
Rustic Hickory Furniture Co.
*Porch, Lawn
and Cottage Furniture.*
Dover Publications, 1991.

Mack, Daniel.
Making Rustic Furniture.
New York: Sterling/Lark, 1992.

Mack, Daniel.
*The Rustic Furniture
Companion.*
New York: Lark, 1996.

Craft and woodworking books available from:

CHESTER BOOK COMPANY
4 Maple Street
Chester, CT 06412
tel: **800-858-8515**

CAMBIUM BOOKS
PO Box 909
Bethel, CT 06801
tel: **203-426-6481**
e-mail: **cambium@ctconnect.com**

LINDEN PUBLISHING
336 W. Bedford #107
Fresno, CA 93711
tel: **800-345-4447**
website: **www.lindenpub.com**

EAIA BOOKS
1321 Cypress-N. Houston Rd.
Cypress, TX 77429

LARK BOOKS
50 College Street
Asheville, NC 28801
tel: **800-284-3388**
website: **www.larkbooks.com/**

ANTIQUE TOOLS MAGAZINES/JOURNALS

**EARLY AMERICAN
INDUSTRIES ASSOCIATION**
PO Box 2128
ESP Station
Albany, NY 12220

FINE TOOL JOURNAL
PO Box 4001
Pittsford, VT 05763
tel: **800-248-8114**

CRAFT/WOODWORKING MAGAZINES

AMERICAN CRAFT
PO Box 3000
Denville, NJ 07834

THE CRAFTS REPORT
700 Orange Street
Box 1992
Wilmington, DE 19899
tel: **302-656-2209**

WOODSHOP NEWS
Pratt Street
Essex, CT 06426
tel: **203-767-8227**

GALLERIES SPECIALIZING IN NEW RUSTIC WORK

TWIGZ N THINGZ
5449 Main Street
Windham, NY 12496
tel: **518-734-5877**

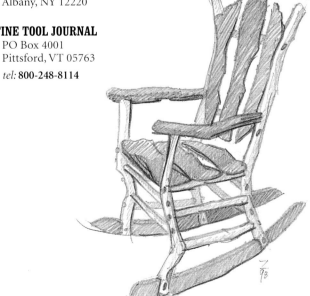

METRIC CONVERSION CHART

Inches	CM		Inches	CM
1/8	0.3		20	50.8
1/4	0.6		21	53.3
3/8	1.0		22	55.9
1/2	1.3		23	58.4
5/8	1.6		24	61.0
3/4	1.9		25	63.5
7/8	2.2		26	66.0
1	2.5		27	68.6
1 1/4	3.2		28	71.1
1 1/2	3.8		29	73.7
1 3/4	4.4		30	76.2
2	5.1		31	78.7
2 1/2	6.4		32	81.3
3	7.6		33	83.8
3 1/2	8.9		34	86.4
4	10.2		35	88.9
4 1/2	11.4		36	91.4
5	12.7		37	94.0
6	15.2		38	96.5
7	17.8		39	99.1
8	20.3		40	101.6
9	22.9		41	104.1
10	25.4		42	106.7
11	27.9		43	109.2
12	30.5		44	111.8
13	33.0		45	114.3
14	35.6		46	116.8
15	38.1		47	119.4
16	40.6		48	121.9
17	43.2		49	124.5
18	45.7		50	127.0
19	48.3			

INDEX